MW01054467

# ALFRED MYLNE

## The Leading Yacht Designer: 1896–1920

**IAN NICOLSON C.ENG. F.R.I.N.A. HON M.I.I.M.S.
WITH DAVID GRAY C.ENG. MRINA SNAME MYDSA**

AMBERLEY

First published 2015

Amberley Publishing
The Hill, Stroud
Gloucestershire, GL5 4EP

www.amberley-books.com

Copyright © Ian Nicolson and David Gray 2015

The right of Ian Nicolson and David Gray to be identified as the Author
of this work has been asserted in accordance with the
Copyrights, Designs and Patents Act 1988.

ISBN 978 1 4456 4633 6 (print)
ISBN 978 1 4456 4634 3 (ebook)

All rights reserved. No part of this book may be reprinted
or reproduced or utilised in any form or by any electronic,
mechanical or other means, now known or hereafter invented,
including photocopying and recording, or in any information
storage or retrieval system, without the permission in writing
from the Publishers.

British Library Cataloguing in Publication Data.
A catalogue record for this book is available from the British Library.

Typeset in 10pt on 12pt Sabon.
Typesetting and Origination by Amberley Publishing.
Printed in the UK.

# CONTENTS

Foreword   4

Introduction   5

| Chapter | Sailing vessels and Mylne Design Number | Length overall | |
|---|---|---|---|
| 1 | *Myrtle* No. 64 | 18 ft | 7 |
| 2 | Sailing Boat Designed for Capt. John Hope No. 50 | 20 ft | 13 |
| 3 | Northumberland Class No. 63 | 20 ft | 16 |
| 4 | *Sea Mouse* No. 60 | 21 ft 2 in. | 19 |
| 5 | *Maid of Lorn* No. 154 | 24 ft | 22 |
| 6 | *Mungo* No. 149 | 24 ft 10 in. | 29 |
| 7 | *Myfanwy Bach* No. 125 | 27 ft | 34 |
| 8 | *Seagull* No. 75 | 29 ft 9 in. | 40 |
| 9 | *Kelpie* No. 98 | 30 ft 6 in. | 44 |
| 10 | *Apache* No. 169 | 31 ft ⅜ in. | 51 |
| 11 | Dublin Bay 21-Foot Star Class No. 80–84 | 32 ft 6 in. | 55 |
| 12 | R. North of Ireland Y.C. Island Class No. 193 | 39 ft 5 in. | 63 |
| 13 | *Sentinel* No. 55 | 40 ft | 69 |
| 14 | *Vladimir* No. 106 | 40 ft 6 in. | 74 |
| 15 | *Aline* No. 167 | 42 ft 4 in. | 79 |
| 16 | Clyde One Design No. 41 | 50 ft | 86 |
| 17 | South Coast One Design No. 85 | 57 ft 4 in. | 92 |
| 18 | *Javotte* and *Kate* Nos 162 and 162A | 60 ft | 105 |
| 19 | *Ostara* No. 161 | 75 ft 2 in. | 111 |

**Power Boats**

| | | | |
|---|---|---|---|
| 20 | Motor Dinghy No. 171 | 14 ft 6 in. | 117 |
| 21 | Kelvin Launch No. 182 | 20 ft | 119 |
| 22 | *Amazon* No. 174 | 39 ft 6 in. | 124 |
| 23 | *Etive* No. 217 | 45 ft | 129 |
| 24 | *Narwhal* No. 61 and *Narana* No. 47 | 50 ft and 51 ft | 134 |
| 25 | *Galma* No. 150 | 60 ft 4 in. | 142 |
| 26 | *Spanker* (later *Lotos*) No. 131 | 82 ft | 148 |
| 27 | *Sea King II* No. 248 | 127 ft 7 in. | 153 |

# FOREWORD

In early 2007, I had the great fortune to start one of the biggest adventures of my life, with the purchase of the design business of A. Mylne & Co. from Ian Nicolson. It was a chance encounter with Ian, and a decision of my heart rather than my head, to purchase one of the oldest yacht design studios in the world, since I was largely buying the business sight unseen.

Once we had emptied the Mitchell Library in Glasgow of the entire archive, we set about the extensive task of digitising and cataloguing the 7,000+ drawings, and 600+ designs, discovering on a daily basis the beauty and depth of the design work of Alfred Mylne and his successors.

At this time, we also started to make contact with the owners of Mylne yachts in the United Kingdom and around the world. We have now confirmed the existence of over 200 Mylne-designed yachts still sailing, undergoing restoration and a few looking for a new owner. It is always a pleasure to speak with an owner who has a technical question, or who we can help with information from our archive. They are always enthusiastic, and proud of the heritage of their yacht.

In 2009, we inaugurated the first Mylne Classic Regatta on the Clyde, which confirmed our belief that we were now the keepers of something very special to a lot of people. There are many wonderful old boats in the world, but to own a Mylne is to own a true classic.

For the first time, we now have this book detailing the design philosophy and thinking behind the world's most beautiful pre-war yacht designs. The author, Ian Nicolson, was a partner in the firm for nearly fifty years, and knows more than anyone what it took to be a yacht designer in the days when the art trumped science, and computers had yet to be invented.

I hope, like me, you will find this journey into the world of Alfred Mylne and his yacht designs as intriguing as it is surprising – mostly because every time I think I have come up with a clever way to achieve something, I find Alfred Mylne or one of his contemporaries were thinking the same thought over one hundred years ago.

David Gray, C.ENG. MRINA SNAME MYDSA
Mylne Yacht Design (A. Mylne & Co.)
April 2015, Limekilns, Scotland

# INTRODUCTION

Beautiful boats last a long time, but ugly ones die young. This is one of the reasons why there are so many Alfred Mylne-designed yachts still sailing, even though some of them are well over one hundred years old. The photo of *Tigris* on the cover says it all. She is a typical example, being far over one hundred years old and still being raced hard in every kind of weather. In the tempest that hit the 2008 Regatta Royales in the Mediterranean, one of them sailed through unharmed, while two yachts sank and the International 12-Metre *France* lost her mast.

It was in 1896 that Alfred Mylne set up his yacht design office in Glasgow, aged twenty-four. He had worked with George Watson, who has the reputation of being the first person to use science as well as art to design yachts. Young Mylne kept up this trend and was also a strong innovator.

Boat design features that are widely believed to be quite new are found in early Mylne designs from well over one hundred years ago. Some of his yachts had fin keels with bulbs in the early 1900s, and some had roller-furling headsails before the First World War started in 1914. At that time, he was designing motor yachts with universal joints between the engine and the stern tube. The aim here is to deal with light flexible hulls and engine line-up problems. The fashion for this type of shaft joint came back in the 1980s, amid acclamation about this 'new' idea!

In 1911, Alfred Mylne, with his brother Charles, bought the boatyard at Ardmaleish Point on Bute, so that yachts of his design could be built under his supervision. Until 1975, when the yard passed out of the Mylne ownership, it was called Bute Slip Dock, and this is where so many breathtaking beauties were built. They were built of wood, because in those days that was the only material used for yacht building, apart from a tiny number made of steel and an even smaller number of aluminium. The yard employed around thirty men, mainly highly skilled shipwrights, but also including a blacksmith who made the fittings for on deck and on the spars. There was also a full-time rigger who doubled as a paid hand on a Mylne yacht in summer.

When the First World War broke out the yard turned to building small naval craft and then flying boats. These aircraft had a lot of yacht building technology in them. For instance, there were cockpit coamings to support machine guns made from ultra-thin wood laminations and some screws holding the wood layers together were only one eighth of an inch long.

Before the First World War began and between the two world wars, Alfred Mylne designed a wide variety of yachts including International 6-, 8- and 12-Metre yachts, plenty of which are still going strong. Racing successes were frequent, helped by the fact that the same owners returned repeatedly for replacement yachts when age and advancing technology outdated earlier craft. Alfred Mylne was a skilled helmsman and he owned an old Clyde Thirty Class called *Medea* which he raced against the new International 8 Metres when they first came out. The design drawings of this yacht are included in this book.

Like all his generation, he was friendly with the small group of successful British designers, but especially with William Fife. Only three yachts were built in the Fife yard at Fairlie which were not designed by Fife. These were the Mylne-designed 79-foot *Mariella*, now in Antigua, the Mylne 54-foot *Irina VII* (ex *Sonas*) now in France, and the Laurent Giles-designed 12-Metre *Flica II*. These yachts show their pedigree because they have been wonderfully well restored.

In the autumn of 1939, the Second World War broke out and Will Fife decided to stop working, as he was getting old and tired from the tough years running a busy boatyard. He phoned Alfred Mylne and said:

'I am retiring, and I would like to give you a keep-sake. What would you like?'

The answer was: 'I know that if this war had not started you would have built an International 12-Metre. I would like the half model of her which you made.' This is why in the collection of Mylne half models, there is only one yacht which is by another designer.

The Mylne archives include a set of exceptional half models, including a trimaran and a motor yacht which was sailed (with some engine usage) from Britain to New Zealand. The oldest half model dates from 1894, when Alfred Mylne built himself an 18-foot half-decker in a second floor flat in the West End of Glasgow. She was lowered out of a window, using a temporary gantry, and onto a cart waiting below one evening. By breakfast time next morning she was at Rothesay, having been taken there by the nightly steamer. What a pity that with all the modern innovations in transport and technology, it now takes ten times as long to move boats, or almost anything, anywhere.

Some of the Mylne half models are in the Greenwich National Maritime Museum but most are not on display, being kept in a closed store. There are also Mylne half models in the Royal Northern and Clyde Yacht Club, in the Royal Thames Yacht Club in London and in other yacht clubs round the world.

In 1945, Alfred Mylne retired and handed the design office in Glasgow and the yacht building yard on Bute to his nephew, who had the same name and has always been known as A. M. the Second. The Mylne family lineage was broken when Ian Nicolson joined the Second Alfred in 1959. When Alfred Mylne the Second died in 1979, Ian took over the design office till 2007, when A. Mylne & Co. was sold to David Gray of Ace Marine of Limekilns in Fife, Scotland.

A. Mylne & Co., with Ace Marine, has lots of aces in its hands. The extensive archives, one of the oldest in the world, has been digitised. This means that plans of yachts can be sent out at short notice with technical back-up to anyone who wants to restore or build a wooden boat, from a dinghy to a launch, and from a racing machine to a super-yacht. This enhanced service covers all aspects of yacht building and rebuilding, as there are naval architects with expertise ranging from traditional boatbuilding and repairs to the latest technology.

Anyone who is fed up with the current ugly boxy floating caravans, and wants a yacht which will turn heads even in San Tropez or Antigua, or wherever beauty is appreciated, now has a vast choice of boats from the Mylne archives. Among other assets, these traditional yachts do not broach downwind or up, they do not have horrible weather helms, even when they heel to a gust, and they have a cosy, comfortable feel down below. It is no wonder that so many owners of Mylne-designed craft are so enthusiastic about these boats.

Among the Mylne boats currently being rebuilt are the 56-foot *Chicane* in Bermuda, the six yachts of the Dublin Bay 24-foot (waterline) class in Brittany and the International 6-Metre *Kyla* in Le Havre. The teak 59-foot *Eilidh* has undergone a rebuild in France and *Trefoil* has had a brilliant rebuild in Bute, while the International 8-Metre *Helen* has been renewed in Cornwall.

The available expertise for building or rebuilding extends right through the process. For instance the replica International 12-Metre *Kate*, 60-foot overall and looking superb with her laid pine deck, was launched a few years ago in the Caribbean and won her first race on the water and on handicap. Her lines and sail plan are as designed by Alfred Mylne the First, but her whole construction plan is new, thoroughly modern and in line with the current 12-Metre Rule.

It is now possible to buy prints of Mylne-designed yachts and there is a special limited edition in colour of some of the outstanding yachts. What better present is there, for the owner or crew who 'has everything'?

More information about the Mylne dynasty is available on the website www.mylne.com.

# CHAPTER 1

*Myrtle*

18-foot Falmouth Restricted Class. Design No. 64
Length overall: 18 ft; 5.49 m.
Length waterline: 17 ft, 6 in.; 5.33 m.
Beam: 7 ft, 2 in.; 2.18 m.
Draft: 5 ft; 1.52 m.
Sail area: Various.

Over a hundred years after she was built, this yacht is still winning races. Lots of them. Boat for boat she comes in ahead of yachts twice her length, in spite of the virtually inflexible rule that the larger the yacht, the faster she is. It is little wonder that *Myrtle* has been rebuilt and that, a century after she was first put together, a sister-ship is under construction. Of course, such a stunning performance does not come without work and attention to detail. For instance, in the autumn of 1930, a new piece of lead some 3 cwts (152 kg) in weight was added in the deadwood above the ballast in order to increase the stability.

There are several reasons why this yacht is so fast, the principle one being the size of the sails. The height of the mainsail, 34 feet (10.63 m) above the deck, is a contributing factor, as is the depth of keel. Long before the wider world appreciated that for speed to windward one wants lots of height aloft and a deep depth below, Alfred Mylne knew this secret, and used to regularly.

Many decades before other designers started producing wide boats, with the crew sitting well outboard to enhance the yacht's stability, Alfred Mylne was using this technique, as the boat's design shows. In the era when she was built, skinny narrow boats were usual in Britain, but in contrast *Myrtle* is, relatively speaking, wildly beamy.

A boat like this is going to throw a lot of water about when racing to windward, so to keep plenty of the sea where it belongs there are wide side decks, and the fore-end of the cockpit is almost back amidships. When water does come inboard in this yacht, it goes into the low bilge and not into the lee bilge where it would slosh about and slice the stability.

The construction plans are full of subtleties. To keep water from getting below, the cockpit coamings sweep round at the fore-end in a bold bend. This would be hard to fabricate in many woods, but American elm is specified and when moderately steamed it will take this bend without much sweating and swearing. It is a fairly light wood but tough, which is a quality needed on a racing yacht.

Looking at the construction plan shows all sorts of cunning ideas that have been reinvented in the years since *Myrtle* first went afloat. For instance, she has a mast step made in the form of a channel bar, with a 1 × ¹⁄₁₆-inch (25 × 1.5 mm) steel strap passing under the step then diagonally upwards and outboard each side onto a chain plate. One chain plate bolt holds the top of the strap on each side and it is arguable that nothing on any boat should be held by a single bolt. However, designing racing boats is a series of calculated risks, and this is just one of those gambles. Normally three fastenings in any component is the minimum acceptable and five are preferred, to be safe.

The chain plates are tapered in thickness from ¼ inch (6 mm) at the top, down to ⅛ inch (3 mm) at the bottom. This sort of subtle craftsmanship was possible when many yacht yards had their own full-time blacksmiths. It will be interesting to see when modern yacht builders clamber back to such a fine level of production and fit tapered chain plates.

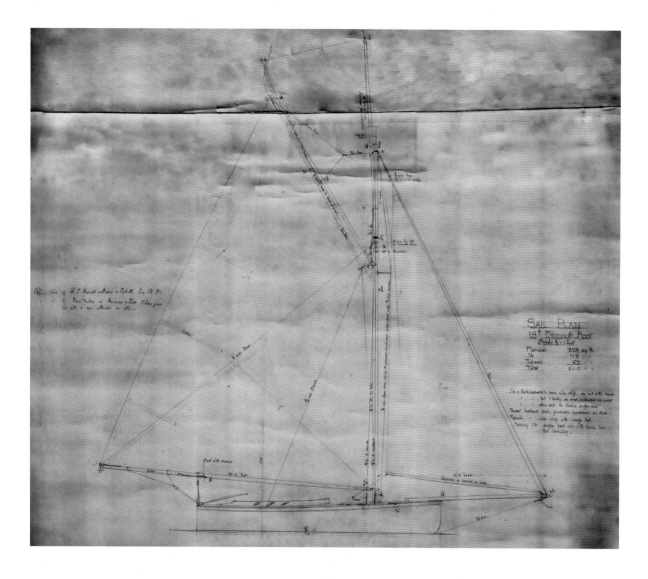

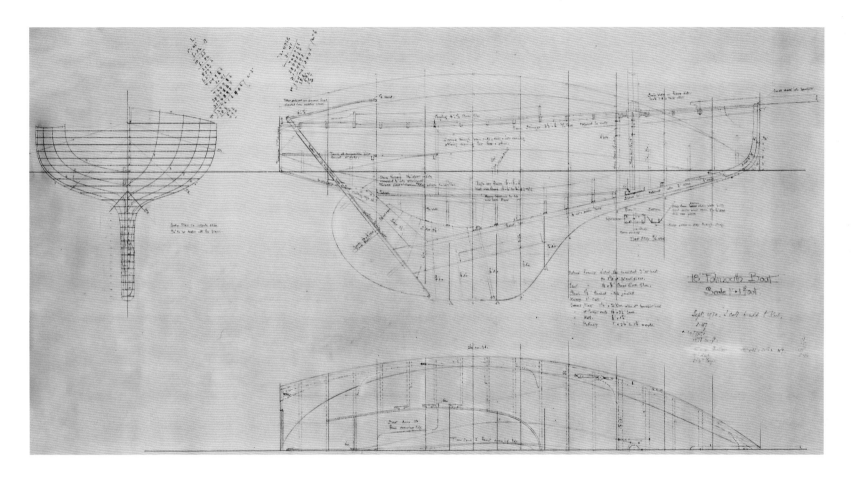

The loads on the spars must be high with such a broad spread of sail, and the thrust aft on the bowsprit cannot be safely held by the single vertical bolt at the aft end. To get over this problem in a simple inexpensive way, the designer has called for a small recess in the bottom of the bowsprit which takes a matching rectangle of wood on top of the stem.

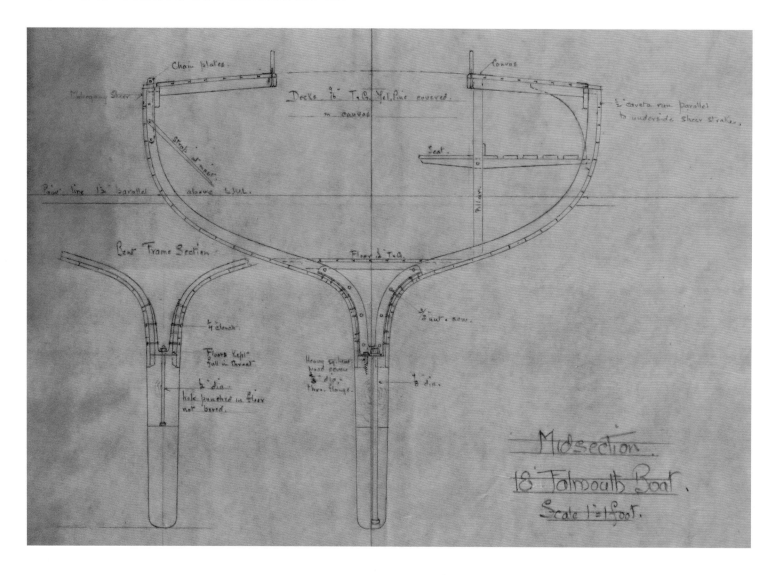

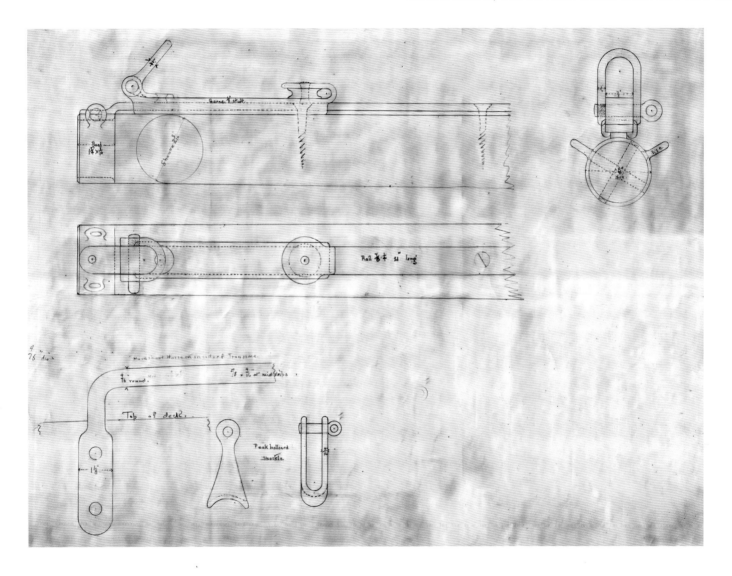

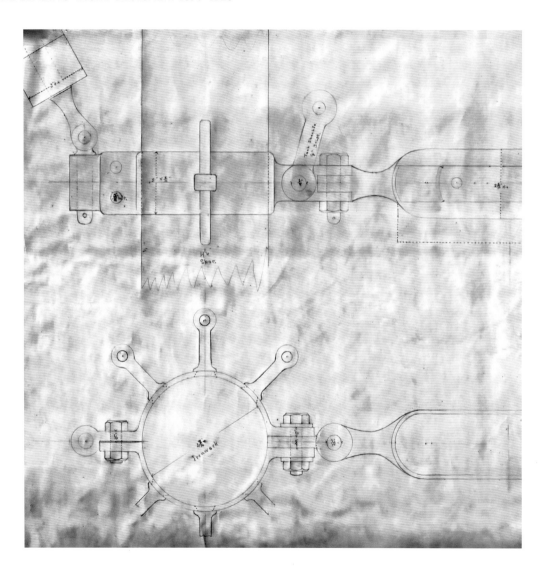

# CHAPTER 2

Sailing boat designed for Capt. John Hope of the Royal Navy
Length overall: 20 ft; 6.1 m.
Length waterline: 17 ft; 5.18 m.
Beam: 6 ft, 11 in.; 2.11 m.
Draft: 1 ft, 7 in. and 4 ft, 2 in.; 483 mm and 1.27 m.
Sail areas: Main 215 sq. ft, Jib 55 sq. ft; 19.97 sq. m. and 5.11 sq. m.

Captain John Hope left the Royal Navy due to ill health, and he lived on the Solway Firth, south-west Scotland, where the waters are shallow. For his home waters and his reduced strength he needed a boat that had a small draft and was easy to handle. Also, she had to be extra safe for someone who was not strong.

Alfred Mylne designed a rugged little yacht which could lie on the beach at low tide, thanks to her long, strong ballast keel. She has a gentle slope on the bottom of the stem and forward deadwood, as well as the small tilt up on the bottom of the forward end of the ballast keel. As a result, this yacht can go aground safely even when sailing quite fast, provided the sea bed is sandy, which it is in the Solway area.

A yacht that is designed to take the ground needs above-average strength, so there are grown frames with two bent timbers between. This construction can be described as typical of Clyde-built yachts and it is more expensive than having all bent timbers, but the Hope family were not poor, and clearly wanted a boat which could stand up to the conditions where they sailed. The ballast keel extends back to form the bottom pivot of the rudder and at first sight its weight seems biased too far aft, when looked at in elevation. However, a detailed study of the drawings shows that the ballast is widest forward of amidships, and the aft end of this keel is quite narrow.

The bottom of the transom is immersed slightly, a typical Mylne feature. It was probably designing for the 19/24 racing class that taught Alfred Mylne the advantages of having a small amount of transom immersion to get the best all-round speed in different wind strengths. However, some lesser designers have never learned this lesson, even many decades after Alfred Mylne died. It pays to study the works of the 'Masters'.

A 5/8-inch (15 mm) thick galvanised steel centre-plate gives this boat the ability to sail to windward. However, it does not go down deep, because if it did so there would be little of the plate left inside the casing and then the plate might bend when the yacht ran aground, especially if there was a tide running hard athwartships, setting the boat sideways. This is always a worry with metal centreboards, and once bent they cannot be hauled back up inside the casing. Doing a repair of a bent metal centreboard is seldom easy, quick or cheap.

One disadvantage of having a centreboard in any yacht likely to touch the ground is that stones and suchlike can get into the centreboard slot and sometimes jam the board. However, this is a risk where the seabed is shingle and stones. Sand is seldom much trouble in this respect.

It is important to have a high rig and a deep keel for the best performance to windward, but this boat is a day sailer, for pottering about afloat, not a racing machine.

Thanks to her ample beam, substantial outside ballast and low rig, this yacht should sail upright and will not need sitting out in normal conditions. Her cockpit is narrow so the side decks are wide and the cockpit starts aft of the mast. As a result, even in gusty weather the sea should stay in its

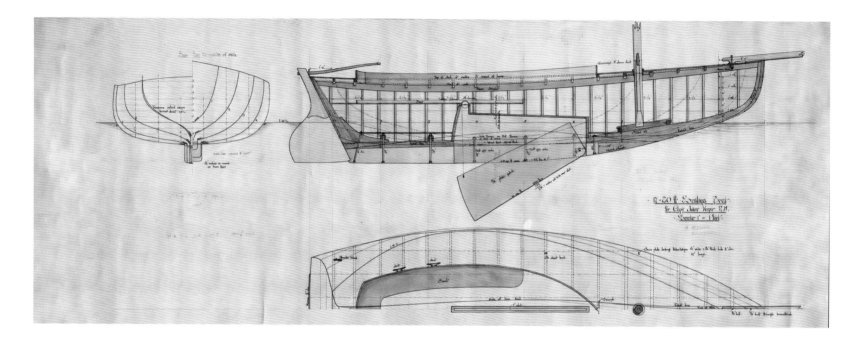

place and not invade the cockpit, even if lots of water tumbles on deck. Having cockpit coamings which curve in to the centre-line at the fore-end is a good way of keeping incoming waves out of the boat. It is typical of Alfred Mylne, who loved beautiful yachts, that he has designed the aft end of the cockpit in a bold curve. If the aft coaming had been drawn straight across athwartships, this would have saved a little money but would have been plainer, and who wants a plain yacht?

It is a characteristic of the times during which this yacht was built, before the First World War, that simple yet clever tricks were used to save money for the builder and owner. For instance, the jib tack was a rope loop which fitted over the outer end of the bowsprit. These days even the cheapest dinghy has a metal fastening such as a snap shackle to secure the headsail tack. And instead of having a sampson post or large cleat for the mooring, the aft end of the bowsprit is shaped to take the mooring loop.

The owner of this yacht had an interesting ancestor, the Earl of Selkirk, who as a young child was nearly kidnapped by the famous Scottish-American privateer, John Paul Jones. This far-ranging seaman came ashore near the family home but found the place deserted, so he bundled the silverware he discovered on the breakfast table into a sack and rushed back to his ship. A long time later, the silver service was found in the sack, well hidden in a hole in the ground, and with the tea leaves still in the teapot.

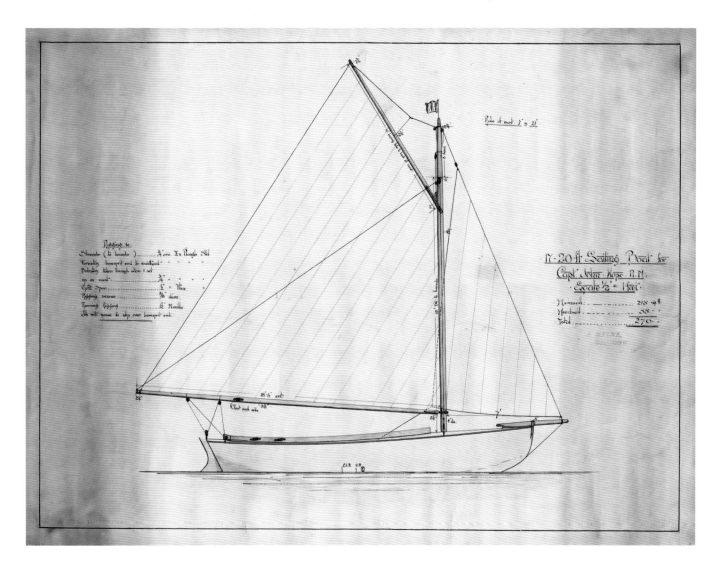

# CHAPTER 3

Northumberland Class

Design No. 63

Length overall: 20 ft; 6.10 m.

Length waterline; 17 ft; 5.18 m.

Beam: 6 ft, 3 in.; 1.905 m.

Draft: 3 ft, 2 in.; 965 mm.

Sail area: 250 sq. ft; 23.23 sq. m.

This design is a lesson in economical boatbuilding. The overhangs, the part of the boat extending beyond the fore and aft ends of the waterline, are kept short and there is a transom stern. The bow is 'snubbed', and to give the sail plan its necessary fore and aft length there has to be a short bowsprit. These features ensure a low building cost, especially in the days when such costs were often based on a boat's overall length. If one were modernising this boat, one would almost certainly extend the bow to the point where the fore-end of the bowsprit is.

Other ways in which money was saved can be seen by studying the details on the drawings. Instead of a mooring post, often called a 'sampson post', there is a half cleat on the aft end of the bowsprit, over which the mooring eye is slipped. To be doubly safe, sensible owners will secure a thick line through this eye and take it back to tie it tightly round the mast.

The ballast keel is of iron, which tends to be substantially cheaper than lead, but it is not so effective when beating to windward. However, this is often acceptable in a One Design class, since all boats are equal in all respects and it is the crew that makes the difference to the race-winning capacity. The sides of the ballast keel are flat and vertical, meaning it was a quick and simple job to create the keel mould, which took the minimum time and timber, and this is another money-saving feature. The deadwood above the keel is also flat and vertical, saving another chunk of cash.

Many boats built during the pre-1914 era had ballast keels which were lower at the aft end than the fore-end. This was to help steering and reduce the jolt when running aground. However, it was inconvenient when the yacht was laid up ashore as she tended to sit bow down, sometimes to an inconvenient degree. The keel on this boat is the same depth below the water-line at the fore and aft ends, but there is an inch (25 mm) of rounding along the bottom, which will help when tacking. Once laid up ashore, this class will sit more or less upright in a fore and aft direction.

In one respect the design goes for elegance and performance, even though this has added a smidgen to the building costs. The spars are all tapered, even the titchy bowsprit, which goes from 2 ½ inches (62 mm) diameter at the stemhead, down to 2 ¼ inches (56 mm) at the fore-end.

Sails have traditionally been priced according to their area, largely because for many years about half the price of a sail was the cost of the materials used to make it. Consequently, a 10 per cent reduction in area would typically bring the cost down by 5 per cent. This explains in part why the headsail is so small. With its boom along most of the length of the foot, this sail can be made self-taking, which suits anyone sailing single-handed.

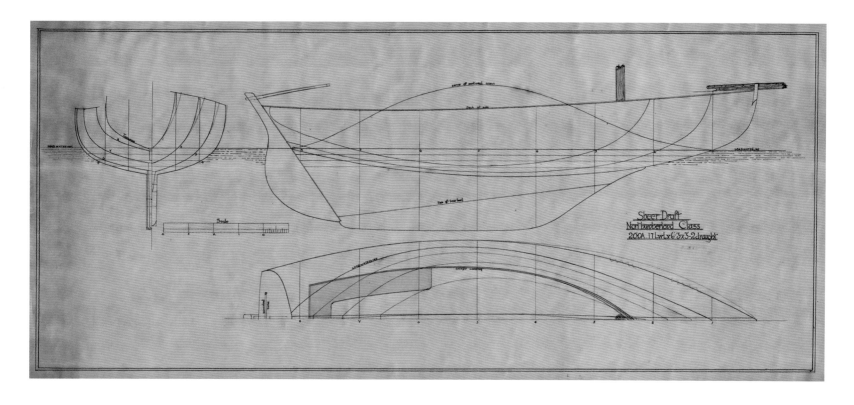

Sheer Draft
Northumberland Class
200A 17 LwL x 6'3 x 3-2 draught

To keep the cost of the standing rigging to a minimum there are just two shrouds and a forestay, as well as the tiny bobstay. The running rigging is also minimalist, with just a single masthead block for the peak halyard and a recessed sheave, but no blocks for the throat halyard. The gooseneck is shown as the old-fashioned type, with the bottom bearing below the horizontal axle pin. This is a poor arrangement and an upper and lower bearing are so much better, reducing wear by much more than half. However, these goosenecks were made of good steel and lasted a long time, in spite of their constantly rusting in way of the bearings, due to the regular wetting and wear every summer afloat.

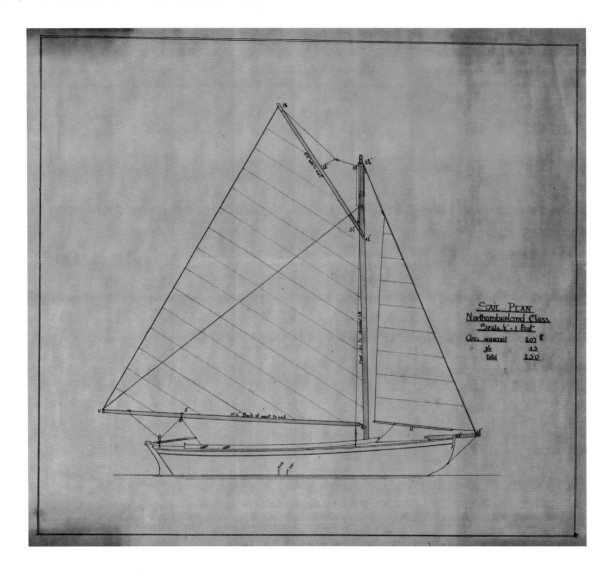

# CHAPTER 4

*Sea Mouse*
Design No. 60
Length overall: 21 ft, 2 in.; 6.45 m.
Length waterline: 16 ft; 4.87 m.
Beam: 6 ft, 6 in.; 1.98 m.
Draft: 1 ft, 7 in. and 3 ft, 11 in.; 483 mm and 1.19 m.
Sail areas: Mainsail 150 sq. ft; Jib 25 sq. ft; Mainsail 13. 94 sq. m, Jib 2. 32 sq. m.
Larger rig: Mainsail 174 sq. ft; Jib 41 sq. ft; Mainsail 16.17 sq. m, Jib 3. 81 sq. m.
Built by McAlisters, Dumbarton, Scotland 1901.

Anyone who wants a day sailer has to think carefully about having a shoal draft boat. There are so many advantages, including: a wider choice of moorings; the ability to work close to the shore when wind or tide are adverse; more creeks to explore; easier slipping and storing each autumn; easier moving by road and so on.

This little boat will not be the fastest yacht going to windward, but she can make good progress by sneaking close along the shore to get the advantages of tidal back eddies and wind shifts round buildings and headlands. She has a very low rig, almost the same as the overall length, and for good progress to windward one of the first things needed is a high rig.

However, this must be the cheapest rig any of us have ever studied. The mast and gaff are short solid spars, so material for them will cost little and be easy to find. The lug mainsail is about the simplest sail anyone can make, with no sail slides and not even the expense of a set of gaff jaws. It is true that in light airs the headsail may need to be coaxed past the gaff fore-end when tacking, but this is a small price to pay for the saving in first costs.

The spars all stow on deck within the length of the yacht, which makes storage ashore, or moving the boat by road, extra easy. Having the forestay back from the stem in the smaller rig is an asset when picking up a mooring. The crew can lie on the foredeck, one hand on the forestay, and reach out for the pick-up buoy, all the while wrapping legs round the mast to avoid falling overboard. With practice, a handy little boat like this can also be brought to a mooring without anyone leaving the cockpit, and in squally difficult conditions the mainsail will come down instantly once the pick-up buoy is on board, thanks to the absence of sail track and slides on the mast.

There are two sail plans, the smaller areas will suit children and the elderly. The larger one is still so small that quite young children will be able to handle both the mainsail and jib. Both are so small that the costs will be low because sails are priced by their area.

Shoal draft boats have to be designed to touch bottom often, and the well-sloped fore-end of the keel is just what is needed, especially as it is combined with a gently-rounded keel toe. When this boat slides up onto a sand-bank, the crew can easily climb over the side and push her off, taking care she does not promptly sail off and leave them stranded. This is where that easily lowered mainsail again comes into its own. Getting it back up once the boat is refloated will be a quick easy job too.

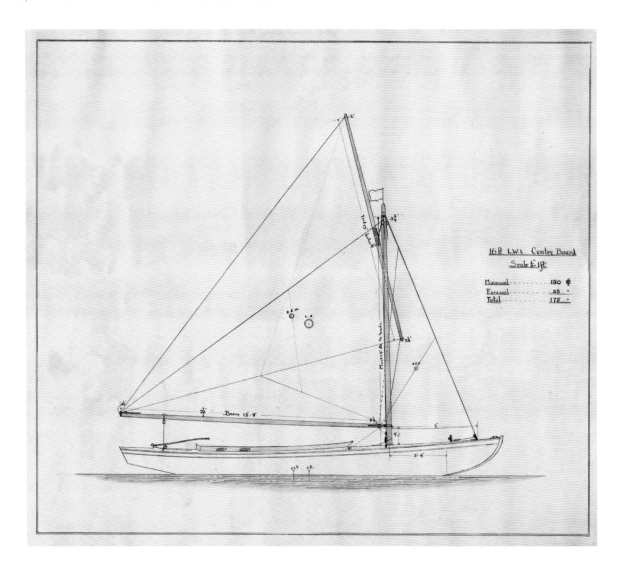

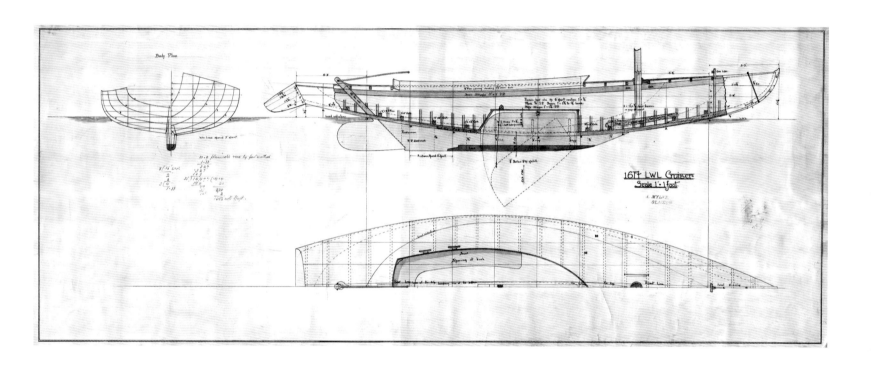

# CHAPTER 5

*Maid of Lorn*
Design No. 154
Length overall: 24 ft; 7.315 m.
Length waterline: 18 ft; 5.486 m.
Beam: 7 ft, 3 in.; 2.21 m.
Draft: 4 ft, 5 in.; 1.346 m.
Sail areas: Main 211 sq. ft, Miz'n 50 sq. ft, Jib 115 sq. ft, Storm jib 36 sq. ft;
Main 19.6 sq. m, Miz'n 4.65 sq. m, Jib 10.68 sq. m, Storn jib 3.34 sq. m.
Builder: A. McKellor, 1908. Canoe stern added 1909.

One recent windy day on the Clyde, when very few boats ventured out, *Maid of Lorn* was seen pounding to windward under headsail and mizzen, making wonderful progress in spite of a wicked short, steep sea. Her owner, Professor John Blackie, was alone on board, having a wonderful sail in his boat that is over one hundred years old. The lovely little *Maid* is lucky in that she has pitch pine planking and teak trim, which explains why she is still going strong, and she has been doubly fortunate to have a dedicated owner who has restored her and then cherished her, year after year.

The *Maid* was built with a transom stern, having her canoe stern added the next year. For a skilled shipwright it is not too difficult to extend a planked boat, provided the designer can work in the extra length by starting well clear of the hull end, and fairing in the addition gently.

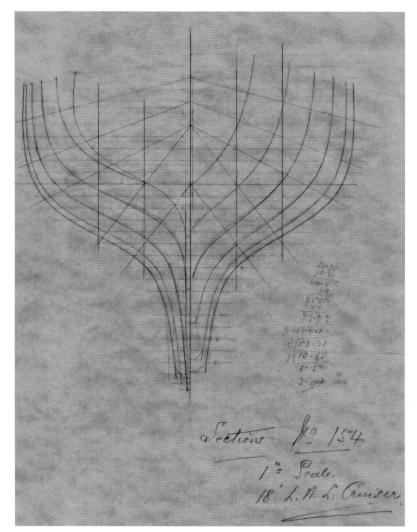

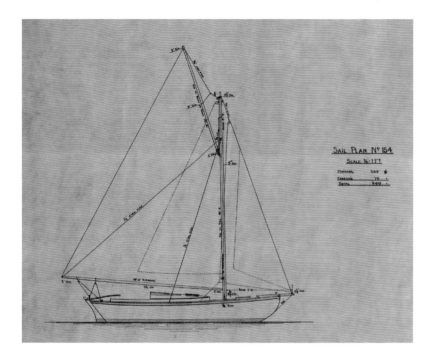

SAIL PLAN Nº 154

The latest sail plan, dated 1994, shows a larger headsail for light winds, and a storm jib which is set on the stem head. Hanking on a heavy weather sail to a portable inner forestay is easier than setting it on the outer end of a bowsprit. The two reefs in the mainsail are 4 feet (1.22 m) deep at the fore-end, but 5 feet (1.52 m) at the aft end. This means that as a reef is taken down the aft end of the boom tilts up, so there is less risk that the boom will drag in the water even in a squall. It also gives a little welcome extra headroom under the boom, a better view to leeward and fractionally moves the centre of effort of the sail plan forward, which reduces any tendency for the boat to have weather helm.

It is easy to realise that this yacht was built when the cost of labour was low. She has a circular fore hatch and a well-rounded cabin top front, two features that take a lot of time and skill to build. The advantage of these curvy fabrications is that they have no corner posts, so sources of shrinkage and leaking are eliminated and varnish lies better when there are no sharp edges. As this fore hatch is so far forward, one of the crew can stand in it when recovering the mooring. There is scarcely room for a mooring strong point forward of the fore hatch, but this does not matter because the aft end of the bowsprit forms a mooring cleat. This is a sensible arrangement, as many owners of Mylne-designed yachts have discovered, since so many sampson posts cause leaks at deck level due to the heavy jerking loads when moored in rough conditions.

The Clyde is made a cheerful place every summer by the presence of this elegant pale green yawl with her richly coloured dark brown sails made of tanned terylene. What a contrast she is to so many modern boxy ugly floating caravans.

In practice the job tends to be easier when the vessel is large, and a careful study of the plans of this yacht's extension, followed by a check of the hull, shows that the two do not exactly match. However, what matters is the final shape and this is lovely, so the shipwrights who built the outreaching canoe stern clearly knew their job.

One reason for lengthening the stern was to fit the mizzen mast, and to balance the extra sail area right aft, the bowsprit was lengthened.

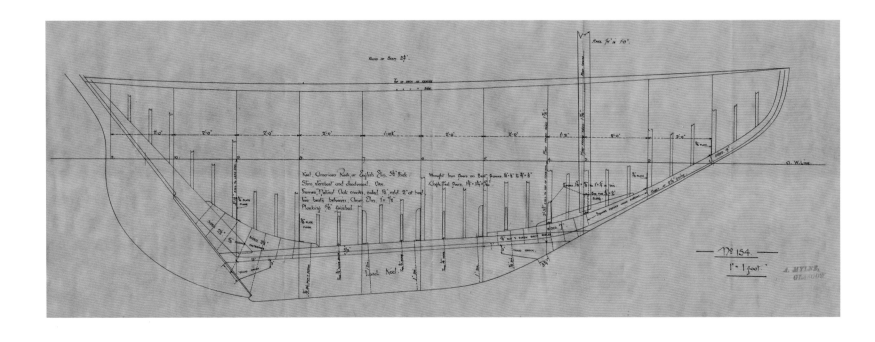

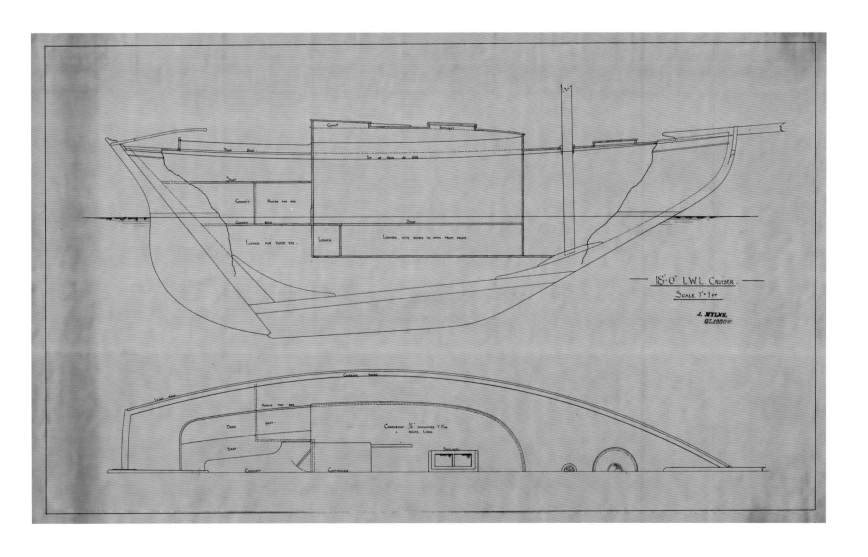

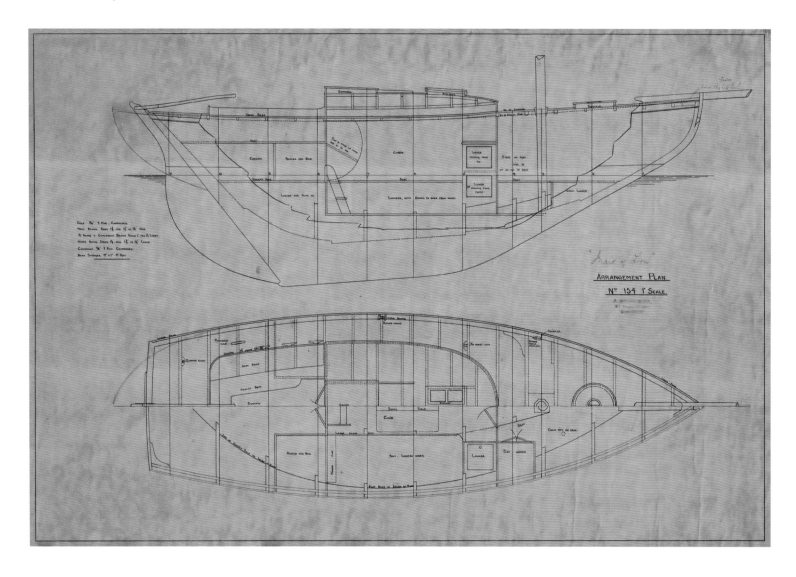

| SPAR | L.O.A | DIMENS & NOTES |
|---|---|---|
| MAIN MAST | | |
| MIZN MAST | 14'-0¾" | 3" ϕ AT BASE 2¾" AT G-NECK 2¼" AT TOP. 12¼" TOP LENGTH 1⅝" ϕ DOWN TO 1⅜" ϕ |
| MAIN BOOM | 16'-9¼" | CONDITION POOR. DIAMS 2¼" FORE END, 3¼" MIDL 2¾" OUTD END |
| MAIN GAFF | 12'-10¾" | DIAMS 2", 3", 2¼". |
| BOWSPRIT | 7'-5½" | NEEDS NET BENEATH / OR ROLR GEAR ETC. DIAMS 4", 3¼", 3" OUTR END. |
| BUMPKIN | | CURVED SHAPE ~ APROX 1¾" OF BOWING. 2½" INBD 2¼" MIDL 2" OUTBD |
| | | |

| SAIL | APROX. DIMENS. | NOTES |
|---|---|---|
| TAND COTN JIB | 19'-2" × 9'-5" × 17'-1" | WORN BADLY. LUFF TWISTD BY WYKEHAM-MARTN GEAR |
| WHITE ELVSM 1966 JIB | 21'-1" × 11'-2" × 19'-11" | NOW HAS LUFF TAPE FOR ROLLER GROOVE. |
| TERYLN JIB ~ CUTCHED | 21'-5" × 11'-6" × 19'-10" | TAND OLD STYLE. L.P. 10'-6" BELIEVED 2ND HAND. |
| STORM JIB | 17'-4" × 7'-7" × 11'-7" | COTN. VERY OLD. UNSAFE. BELIEVED 2ND HAND |
| TANNED MAIN | 13'-4" LUFF. 11'-11" HEAD 15'-6" FOOT. 24'-6" L'CH | THIS SAIL HAS NO FURTHER LIFE IN IT. 19'-2" DIAGL |
| WHITE MAIN | 12'-0" LUFF 11'-6" HEAD 14'-8" FOOT 24'-1" L'CH | THREE SHALLOW REEFS APROX 2'-9" DEEP. BELIEVED 2ND HD |
| TANNED MIZN | 5'-0" LUFF 7'-6" HEAD 7'-8" FOOT 12'-2" L'CH | BADLY WORN. NO FURTHER LIFE IN IT. 8'-5" DIAGL |
| | | |

MIZN BOOM & MIZN GAFF NOT YET SEEN.

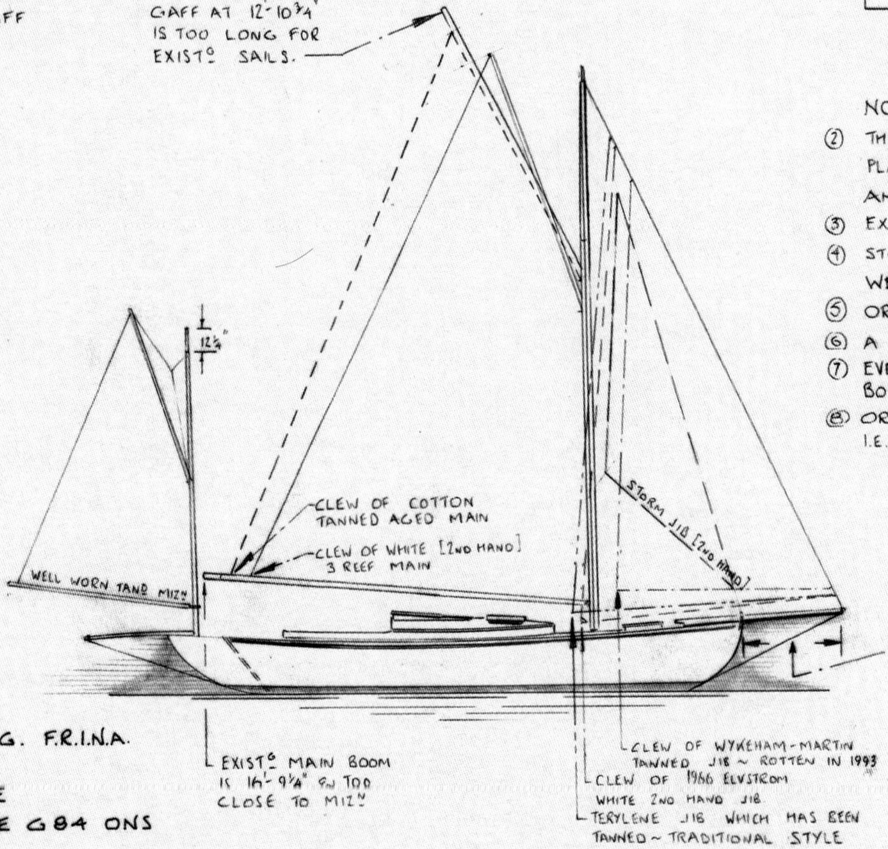

GAFF AT 12'-10¾" IS TOO LONG FOR EXISTG SAILS.
12¼"
CLEW OF COTTON TANNED AGED MAIN
CLEW OF WHITE [2ND HAND] 3 REEF MAIN
WELL WORN TAND MIZN
STORM JIB [2ND HAND]
EXISTG MAIN BOOM IS 16'-9¼" & TOO CLOSE TO MIZN
CLEW OF WYKEHAM-MARTIN TANNED JIB ~ ROTTEN IN 1993
CLEW OF 1966 ELVSTROM WHITE 2ND HAND JIB
TERYLENE JIB WHICH HAS BEEN TANNED ~ TRADITIONAL STYLE


ROUGHLY 4'-4" STEM TO FORE-STAY IS TOO FAR TO REACH & SO SPECIAL GEAR IS NEEDED FOR FORESAIL.

NOTES: (1) SEE 1994 SAIL PLAN.

(2) THIS SAIL PLAN IS BASED ON ORIGINAL 1904 SAIL PLAN PLUS DIMENS TAKEN FROM EXISTG SPARS AND SAILS.

(3) EXISTG SPARS ARE LIGHT FOR MODERN TERLN SAILS

(4) STORM JIB MUST BE VERY EASY TO SET IN BAD WEATHER ~ WITH SHEETG TO LARGE HEADSAIL LEADS.

(5) ORIGINAL SAIL PLAN HAD A TRISAIL.

(6) A BOWSPRIT NET MUST BE CONSIDERED.

(7) EVEN IF A WYKEHAM-MARTIN GEAR IS NEED A BOWSPRIT TRAVELER IS NEEDED.

(8) ORIGINAL SAIL PLAN SHOWS MAIN 285 ϕ, JIB 75 ϕ I.E. TOTAL 360 ϕ


Ian Nicolson C.ENG. F.R.I.N.A.
A. MYLNE & Co
LINNFIELD COVE
DUNBARTONSHIRE G84 ONS


**"MAID OF LORN" AUG 1993**

**PLAN OF EXISTG SAILS ETC.**

**SCALE: ¼" TO 1 FT. DESIGN No 154**

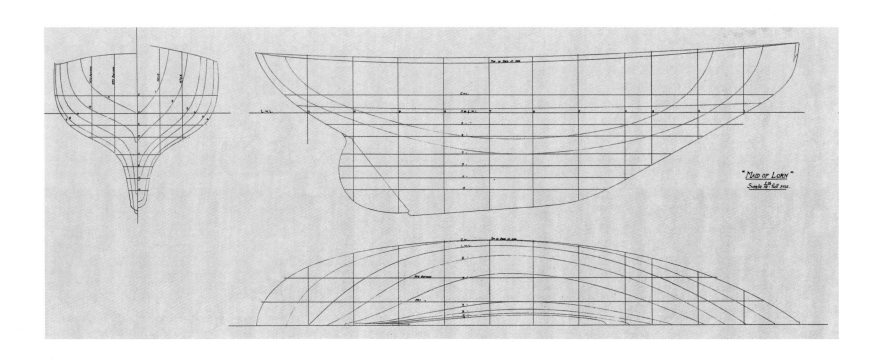

"MAID OF LORN"
Scale ½" full size.

# CHAPTER 6

*Mungo* (later named *Elsbeth III*)
Design No. 149
International 5-Metre Class
L.O.A.: 24 ft, 10 in.; 7.57 m.
L.W.L.: 16 ft, 9 in.; 5.11 m.
Beam: 4 ft, 11 ½ in.; 1.63 m.
Draft: 3 ft, 5 in.; 1.04 m.
Built by Alexander Robertson, Sandbank, Scotland in 1908.

The 1907 Conference of the yachting establishment, which resulted in the International Metre Rule, was a significant event in the history of yacht design and construction. Yachts built to the new rule had to be strong, well-built and able to stand up to hard racing for years, in contrast to the 'raters' and other types of racing yachts built prior to this critical date. Before the coming of the new rule, racing yachts were built as lightly as the designer and builder dared, so they won for a few years then started to leak and deteriorate. This meant they had little value, and, naturally, owners became fed up paying for new craft which had such a short useful life.

In Britain the 'Metre' yachts had to be built to Lloyds Rules and the construction was supervised by a surveyor from Lloyds Register to ensure that the planking, frames, beams and deck etc. were all to the correct thickness, with no skimping allowed. In France, Bureau Veritas acted in the place of the British Lloyds organisation and in Germany Germanischer Lloyd did the same. The rules were laid down in detail and on the whole were easy to follow, with few chances offered to designers and builder to cut corners or reduce the weight. When newly launched, each Metre yacht had a potential life of thirty or fifty years, and many have lasted far longer. This ensured that the boat's value did not drop fast. As a result, old Metre-class racing yachts were bought for coastal cruising and for 'club' racing, which is seldom too serious.

The smallest of the Metre Rule yachts were the 5-Metre size, of which *Mungo* is a good early example. The profile shows a yacht with a shallow draft to suit harbours and racing areas where the water is not deep. If this boat does run aground, her keel profile is 'friendly' with the well-rounded toe of the keel and the slope of the underside of the keel, so running aground should not result in serious damage, unless the sea bed is rocky. This keel profile is easy to launch and haul ashore in a yacht yard where a marine railway is used to get boats out of the water. Before the coming of marinas, this traditional hauling-out gear was universally used. It is still found in some places today, notably in remote areas of the world.

The waterline forward has the common fullness found on early Metre yachts, where the designer aims to have a low wetted surface and short waterline length for light airs, but a longer length when the breeze increases and the yacht heels. The deck line forward is fine, sharp-pointed and intended to cut through waves with little resistance. A counter designed to carry the stern wave well aft has been designed to increase the waterline length and subsequently the top speed when the breeze freshens.

There are fascinating details in the sail plan. For instance, the headsail, which was on a roller furling gear (this was in 1908!) is only about

75 square feet, or 6.97 square metres, so a young teenager could handle it, even though sheet winches were not used when this vessel was racing. A light main boom, with a diameter of only 3 ¼ inches, or 83 mm, along its length, has a roller furling gear to allow the crew to reduce sail swiftly once the topping lift has been set up, and the main sheet eased a little. Such a thin boom needs care to ensure its loads are well spread, and that is why the main sheet has three attachment points.

When this yacht was launched, her larger cousins, the 6- and 8-Metre racing machines, had bowsprits, but *Mungo* does not have this irritating appendage. Anyone who has had to handle sails or anchors on a boat with a bowsprit will have a hearty hatred of these protruding spars. Even the short ones are a menace, often demanding that crew climb out on them to handle sails. Just as annoying, anchors just love to get hitched up on the bobstay or even on the bowsprit shrouds.

In the early 1950s, as a keen young naval architect, my delight was to walk through boatyards and study the yachts laid up. One winter I went into a shed in Burnham-on-Crouch, on the English east coast, and came across four of the 5-Metre class. It was a thrilling moment, as good as finding a well-stuffed wallet with no name or address in it. I got a ladder and looked into each of these delightful boats. Each was a perfect example of the shipwright's craft, with every wood scantling made with rounded edges and corners. The cockpit coamings were so thin and light, yet just strong enough.

These four were almost certainly the last remaining yachts gathered together in the International 5-Metre Class. Their location tells a story, because the River Crouch and the surrounding waters are shallow – when beating against the tide it is essential to go close to the shore. When the yacht runs aground, one or more of the crew will jump overboard and get soaked up to the waist or chest, but they will be able to shove the yacht back into deeper water. However, the type of yacht owner who can afford an expensive boat, and the Metre yachts were always costly to buy new, seldom enjoys getting too wet too often. This may well explain why so few International 5-Metre boats were built.

Between 1907 and 1914, when the First World War started and yacht building almost died till the fighting ended, 328 International 6-Metre yachts were launched, but only forty-one International 5-Metre craft. This was in part because some racing clubs encouraged the 'Sixes', and the chat round the bars was that this class was cheap and fun. To this day the attitude of the flag officers of a club strongly influences the boats raced by that club.

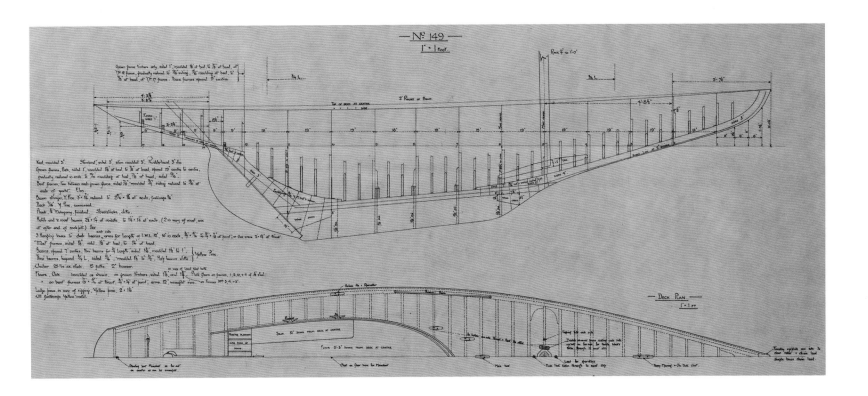

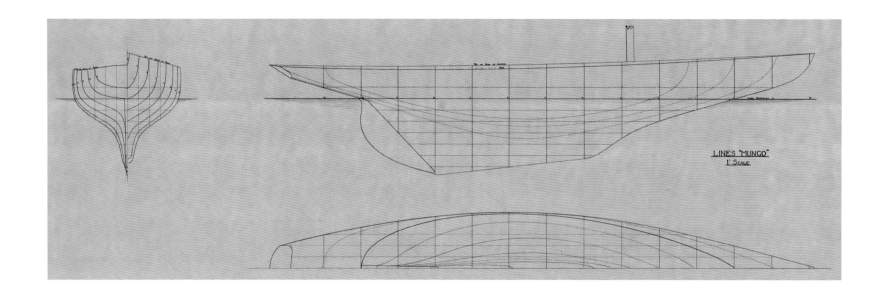

LINES "MUNGO"
1" Scale

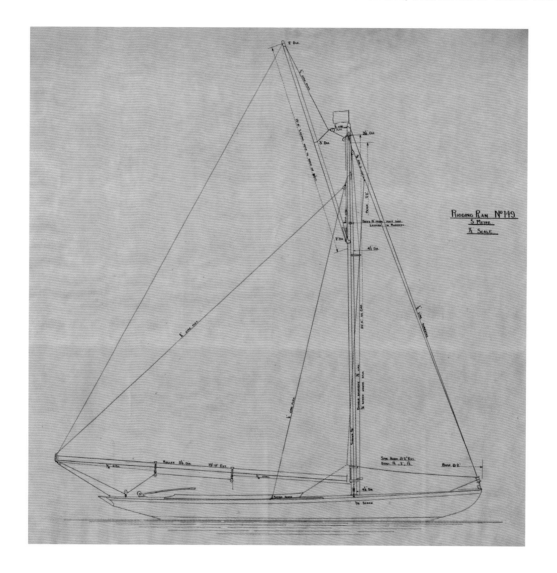

# CHAPTER 7

*Myfanwy Bach*
Design No. 125
Royal Mersey Restricted Class
L.O.A.: 27 ft; 8.23 m.
L.W.L.: 24 ft; 7.32 m.
Beam: 8 ft, 4 in.; 2.54 m.
Draft: 2 ft, 11 in. and 5 ft, 5 ins; 889 mm and 1.65 m.
Built by S. Bond of Birkanhead in 1906.

A 'Restricted Class' is a type of racing boat designed and built within certain limitations such as length, sail area and the thickness of important parts like the planking, deck and frames. The advantage of this style of yacht is that the designer can use his skill and ingenuity to improve on existing yachts, and owners can make alterations to the 'unrestricted' parts of the yacht. With this arrangement, yachts in the class do not get quickly outdated as they do in more 'extreme' types of racing machine. On the other hand, there is an incentive to try out new ideas and constantly improve existing boats. Drilling lightening holes in the cockpit sole can be risky – if there are too many holes or they are too large, someone's foot could plunge through the splintering wood in moments of tension when racing!

This class raced in shallow waters where there is a strong tidal stream. This means that to win a race, it is often essential to sail close

inshore and be ready to tack out when the centreboard rumbles on the sea bed. This board is cunningly designed so that most of it is below the sole in the cabin, making the cabin that much more comfortable and spacious. However, there is plenty of enclosed board area when it is lowered. Also, the angle in the line of the top edges does not extend below the keel, so there should be no water burble here that would slow the yacht. The part of the centreboard that remains inside the casing when it has been lowered is large enough to ensure that the board will not bend if the yacht grounds when sailing fast with a cross-tide.

The hull shape is clever as it should be easy to get this boat back afloat if she goes aground when the centreboard is up, by shoving the bow offshore so that the hull pivots about the deepest point right aft. The waterlines are fine forward with little or no curvature till aft of the mast, but aft they are fully, almost voluptuously swept back to the transom. Mylne knew this would give a good windward performance, but also a tendency to have weather helm. This explains why the original design has a longish bowsprit and why the rudder is a little larger than seen on deep-drafted yachts.

To win races a yacht has to be light. Mylne had to follow that specification laid down by the class rules, which specified the thickness of most hull components. But for the most part it did not say what materials had to be used, so Mylne specified yellow pine for many parts because this is a relatively light wood. He designed the centreboard casing in this material and stated that the bottom part had to be 1 ½ inches thick, as laid down by the rules. He called for the top parts to be only 1 inch thick, no doubt because the rules did not state that the *whole* of the casing had to be 1 ½ inches thick.

When this yacht was built it was rare for sailing boats to have engines, especially ones this size. This meant that if matters got out of hand, in a

sudden squall for instance, the ground tackle was sometimes the last line of hope. In the days when this yacht was built it was symbol of hope, for instance when a charity wanted to have a logo expressing 'HOPE', it used a picture of anchor. It is significant that the Class Rules for the Royal Mersey Class insisted that the main anchor must be at least 40 pounds weight (18.14 kg), and the smaller kedge anchor 20 pounds (9.07kg). So few current yachts have anchors anywhere near this size, and their owners depend on an engine to keep out of trouble.

# SPECIFICATION

## FOR THE

# ROYAL MERSEY RESTRICTED CLASS.

———※———

**Scantlings** shall not be less than the following finished sizes :—

**Keel** $3\frac{1}{2}$ in. thick in wake of centreboard case.

**Transom** $1\frac{1}{4}$ in. sided.

**Timbers**, all steamed, $\frac{3}{4}$ in. x $1\frac{1}{8}$ in. spaced 9 inches centre to centre at heels.

All timbers to be properly joggled into keel where they do not cross same.

**Floors:** not less than four grown floors 3 in. x $2\frac{1}{2}$ in. at throats tapered to ends.

**Iron knees**, galvanized, 2 in. x $\frac{3}{8}$ in. each arm 15 in.   Three to be fitted each side of centreboard case.

**Centreboard case.**   Sides $1\frac{1}{2}$ in. thick.

**Planking.**—One inch finished on boat.

**Clamps**—4 in. x 1 in. tapered to 3 in. at ends.

**Bilge Stringers.**   $3\frac{1}{2}$ in. x 1 in. tapered to 2 in. at ends.

**Decks** caulked not less than $1\frac{1}{8}$ in. finished.   Decks covered with canvas or linoleum, not less than $\frac{7}{8}$ in. finished without covering.

**Deck beams.**   2 in. x $1\frac{3}{4}$ in at centres, fair taper to ends, spaced 18 in.   The 3 Deck beams at mast, fore-end coachroof and after-end cockpit $2\frac{1}{2}$ in. x $2\frac{1}{2}$ in. at centres, fair taper to ends.

**Carlings** for coachroof and cockpit $2\frac{1}{2}$ in. x $2\frac{1}{2}$ in., well kneed.

**Coamings** for coachroof $\frac{7}{8}$ in. finished hardwood.

**Beams coachroof** $1\frac{1}{4}$ in. x $1\frac{1}{4}$ in. spaced 8 in. centres.

**Top of coachroof** $\frac{3}{4}$ in. canvas covered.   No racing hatch in coachroof.   Any skylight not to exceed 30 in. x 20 in. measured inside coamings and to be a fixture and not to be used as a racing hatch.   No sliding hatch to exceed 24 in. x 21 in. in the opening.

**Floor of Cabin and Cockpit** $\frac{7}{8}$ in. thick.

**Cabin seats and risers** $\frac{3}{4}$ in. thick.

**Chain** 25 fathoms $\frac{5}{16}$ in. chain.

**Main anchor** 40 lbs., kedge 20 lbs.   20 fathoms $1\frac{3}{4}$ in. warp.

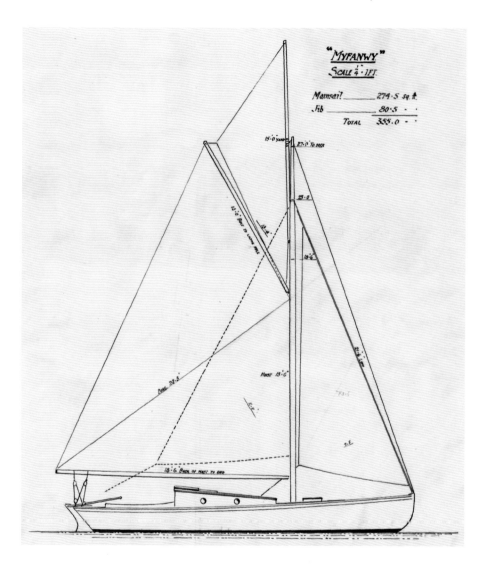

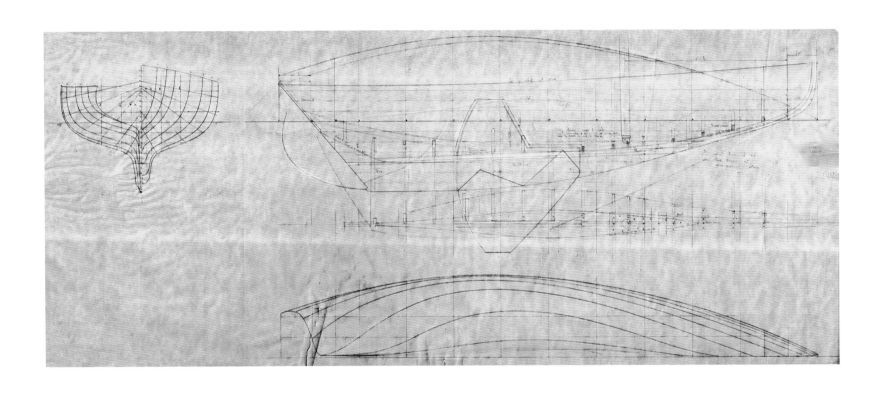

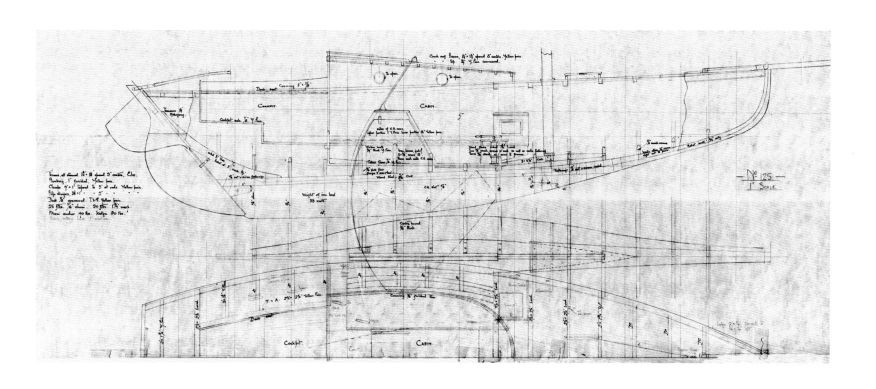

# CHAPTER 8

*Seagull*

Design No. 75

Length Overall: 29 ft, 9 in.; 9.07 m.

Length waterline: 23 ft; 7.01 m.

Beam: 8 ft, 6 in.; 2.59 m.

Draft: 4 ft, 6 in.; 1.37 m.

Sail areas: Mainsail 347 sq. ft; 32. 24 sq. m. Staysail 85 sq. ft; 7.9 sq. m. Jib 116 sq. ft; 10.78 sq. m. Topsail 79 sq. ft; 7.34 sq. m.

Built by A. Malcolm, Port Bannatyne, Isle of Bute, in 1903.

This yacht is still sailing, and not just pottering cautiously about an estuary, but making offshore voyages. It is an often repeated saying that to be successful, a naval architect has to be lucky with his clients. In the same way, a yacht has to be lucky with her successive owners if she is to have a long life. It also helps if she is built well and has design features which ensure she is not overstressed.

The construction plan of *Seagull* has several clues showing why she is still going strong. The draft is relatively shallow, so there are few severe twisting strains on the hull, and the ballast keel is long, deep and strong. The bow overhang is very short and the foredeck is long, with full-width beams right back almost to amidships. By the mast there are two extra strong oak beams to keep the yacht in shape regardless of the stresses imposed by the rig. It is true that the sail area is generous, but on a yacht this size the topsail will seldom be carried in more than moderate winds and it can be hustled down if a squall is seen in the offing.

The lines plan show a typical Mylne shape, with elegant wine-glass sections and a load waterline which is boldly full aft, but forward it is virtually a straight line for the first seven feet, or 2.1 metres. This makes for speed to windward, but a hull which wants to surge up to windward in the gusts. To counteract this, there is generous-sized jib set well forward on a long bowsprit. The buttocks (which are seen in the elevation of the lines plan) at the aft end of the waterline are about 17 degrees to the horizontal, and this is the magic figure which some designers say should not be exceeded if the boat is to be fast. It is based on the idea that the maximum angle that water will adhere firmly to a sloping surface when running up along the underside of the aft end of the hull. Even if this theory is based on nothing more than prejudice, it is undeniably true that buttock lines that slope steeply upwards as they go aft are seldom seen on fast craft.

Amidships the sections have tumblehome, which is not just to give a lovely appearance, though it does that. It also means that when the yacht heels, her waterline width decreases. Since a narrow beam tends to enhance windward performance, it is easy to see why Mylne drew this inward curve amidships.

The cabin top is about as short as it can be, since the sliding hatch has to be about two feet or 600 mm fore and aft if the crew are not to bump their heads going below, but when open the hatch cannot slide beyond the forward end of the cabin top. The cabin top coaming is wonderfully rounded at the fore-end, an expensive but elegant feature.

As originally built, *Seagull* had a super-simple cabin layout, with two settee berths and a pump type toilet right forward, which had less than the standard 38 inches, or 960 mm, of sitting headroom over it. Under the diminutive cabin top there was about 5 foot or 1.524 m of headroom beneath the sliding hatch. A yacht this size is almost bound to be short of stowage space, since she has to carry many items of gear which cannot be compressed in size, such as tools, buckets, mop and boathook, perhaps a bosun's chair, and so on. This means that compared with larger craft, the volume of locker space tends to be less than ideal. In the cockpit there are lockers under the side seats, and these extend right out to the planking. Also, the seats that are the locker tops reach out to the planking, forming useful shelves under the side decks.

Anyone building a boat to these plans today would probably have a self-draining cockpit, and fit an engine beneath. The cabin top might extend a little further forward and aft to make room for a small galley, and a fore hatch over the toilet would be a popular choice. The boom might be a little shorter for easier reefing and to avoid having the boom end out beyond the counter. With hollow spars and good sails, plus of course good helmsmanship, this pretty yacht could give a good account of herself in 'club' racing, and she is likely to be the loveliest yacht in any modern fleet.

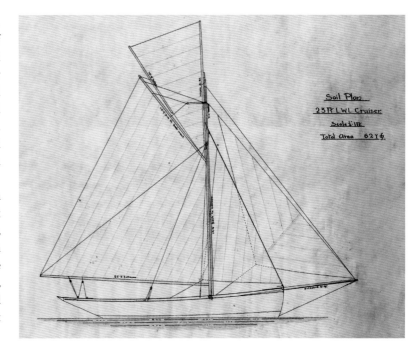

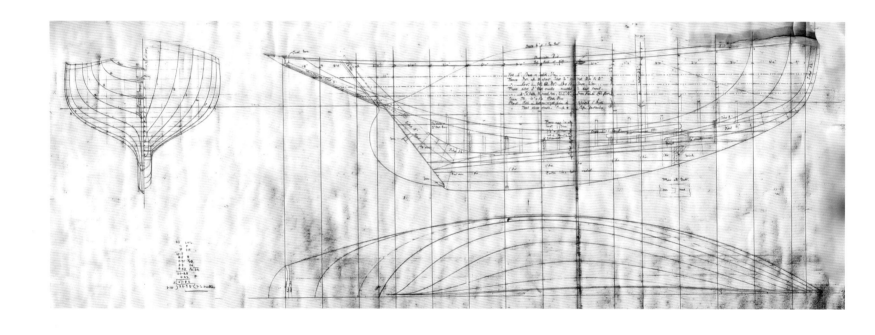

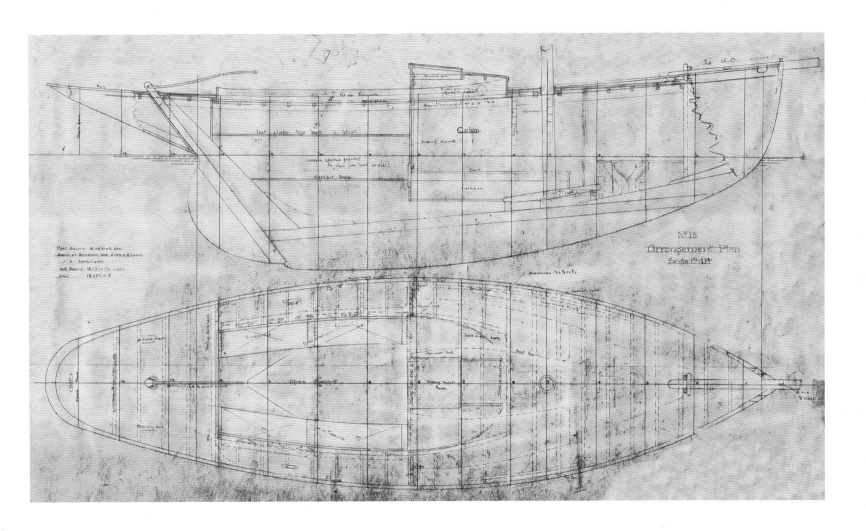

# CHAPTER 9

*Kelpie* (later *Audrey*)

Design No. 98

Length overall: 30 ft, 6 in.; 9.296 m.

Length waterline: 22 ft; 6.706 m.

Beam: 7 ft, 4 in.; 2.235 m.

Draft: 5 ft; 1.524 m.

Sail areas: Mainsail 384 sq. ft; 35.67 sq. m. Jib 193 sq. ft; 17.93 sq. m. Topsail 132 sq. ft; 12.26 sq. m.

Built in 1903.

Lake Windermere is the largest fresh water area in England, but it is surrounded by high hills, so the wind there is often light and fickle. To win races here a yacht must have a large sail area, a small hull wetted surface and minimum weight, so that she accelerates as soon as each puff comes her way.

At sea a yacht is pitched and pummelled, so her attitude to the wind is constantly changing. Under these conditions a good case can be made for having two or three headsails, as many craft did pre-1914. Each sail can be trimmed at a slightly different angle, so that as the yacht jumps about, one sail is always at the best angle to the wind. But on a lake where waves are seldom serious, a single large headsail makes sense.

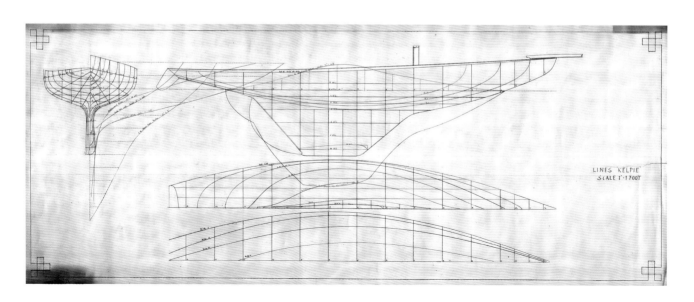

To prevent the wind on the sails 'escaping' under the headsail and boom, from the high pressure on the windward side to the lower pressure on the lee side, both sails are low down. Modern headsails often touch and even drag along the foredeck, but there is a small gap on *Kelpie* to let the crew have a view to leeward when on port tack because they do not have right of way. This yacht was designed in the days before there were plastic windows in sails, giving a view to leeward.

To get the maximum area, the bowsprit curves down at the fore-end, which is acceptable in a yacht that does not go offshore and plunge it's bowsprit under each advancing waves. The boom is so low the helmsman and crew need to be alert to duck down below it during each tack. The fore-end of the boom only just clears the cockpit coaming when it swings outboard.

The current fashion on many racing yachts is for the crew to sit on the weather rail, to use their weight as ballast in the most advantageous location. On many yachts it has been the practice for years to sit with the feet in the cockpit, and in some classes this is all that is allowed. A more effective stance is with the crew sitting facing outboard on the weather side deck, with their feet over the side. At all moderate angles of heel, the crew are further out to windward than the ballast in the keel, so though their combined weight is often much less than that in the metal ballast, their 'weight × distance' effect is sometimes almost as good as the ballast keel.

However, on this yacht the boom is so low that if the crew spent time sitting on the windward side-deck, they would be in danger of being swept overboard during tacking. Instead, at least one of them would be crouching down in the lee side of the cockpit, carefully watching for other yachts' close tacking, so as to shout 'Starboard!' to a port tack boat, or warn the helmsman he would have to tack in good time, or duck to leeward of an on-coming starboard tack yacht.

When looking at the lines plan, phrases like 'racing machine' and 'skimming dish' and 'inshore flyer' come to mind. The flat, shallow hull married to the deep, narrow fin with its bulbous bottom are the traditional features of fast, fun boats. A modern equivalent would be finer forward and probably more difficult to sail, and the keel would be shorter, with a separate rudder. But the shape of this yacht is in several respects astonishingly modern, and with that outsize sail area it is almost certain this boat planed when there was a strong wind from astern.

There is a common expression used to describe the shape of a ballasted yacht when seen from the bow: it is said to have a 'wine-glass section', because the shape is quite like a traditional wine-tipplers favourite container. However, in this case the phrase would be 'champagne-glass section', as the upper part is more flat-bottomed, or as a naval architect would say, the yacht has a flatter floor and a sharper turn of bilge. This is the shape for speed, but it means the interior volume of the hull is much reduced, so few cruising boats can have this mid-ship section.

The gaff jaws are a good example of the careful blacksmith work found on the best yachts of this era. Each piece of wrought iron was made to fit exactly, and tapered away at the ends. Labour costs were cheap before the First World War and there were plenty of blacksmiths, so designers could produce sculptured iron-work and know the end product would look lovely, be light because there was no surplus material, and be functional.

The jaws on the fore-end of the gaff were made of $\frac{1}{16}$ inch (1.5 mm) steel backed up by the arms which held the horizontal pivot pin. These arms were tapered in thickness and width, something seldom seen these days. The fittings were almost always designed round bolts of a standard length and diameter, which were available at all yacht yards and blacksmiths workshops, so there would be no delay getting the fittings made up. To hold the bottom of the topsail yard snug against the back of the mast there are a pair of 'thumbs' screwed in place, so that in practice the topsail and mainsail become like a Bermudan gunter rig.

This yacht is still racing well over one hundred years after she was built. This shows that good design and construction lasts and is to be prized far above other qualities.

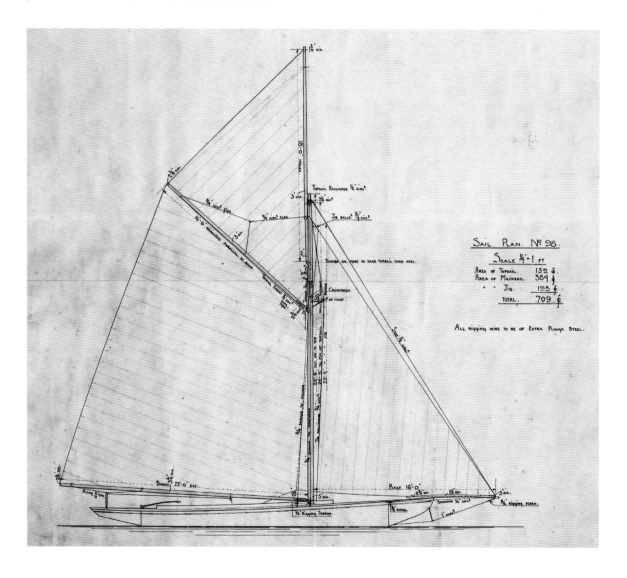

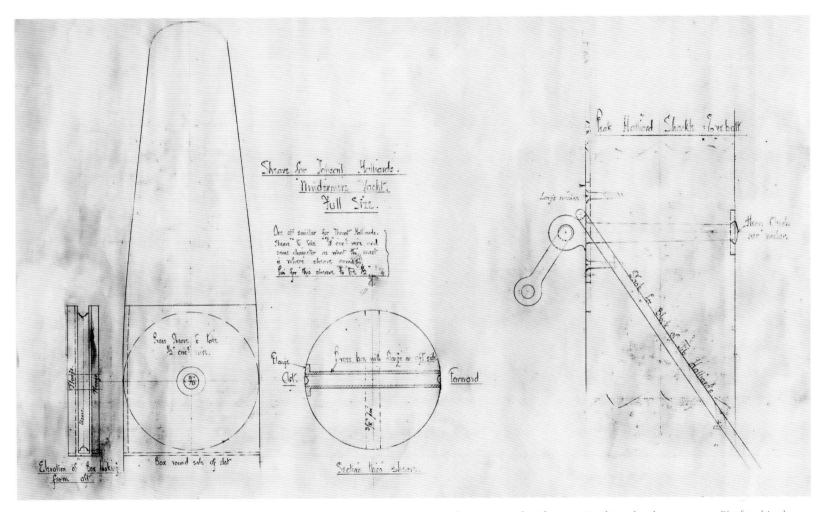

One off similar for Throat Halliard. Sheave to take ⅛ inch circumference wire and same diameter as what the mast is where the sheave comes. Pin for this sheave to be ½ inch.

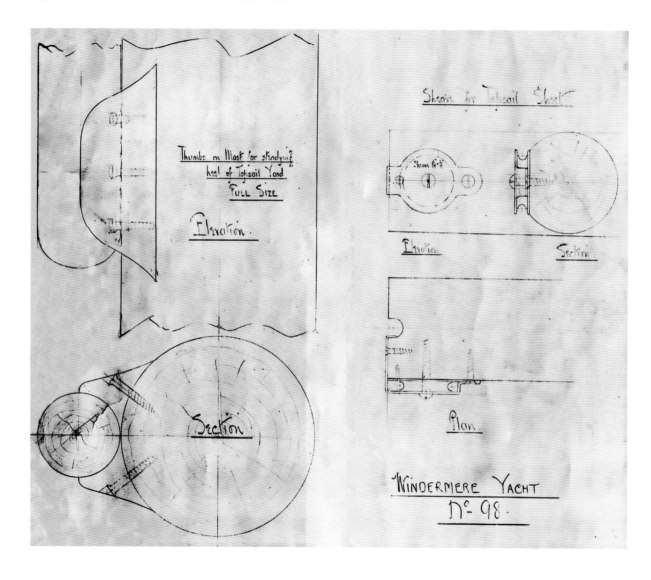

Thumbs on Mast for steadying
heel of Topsail Yard
FULL SIZE

Elevation.

Section

Sheave for Topsail Sheet

Sheave No 8

Elevation                    Section

Plan

WINDERMERE YACHT
N° 98.

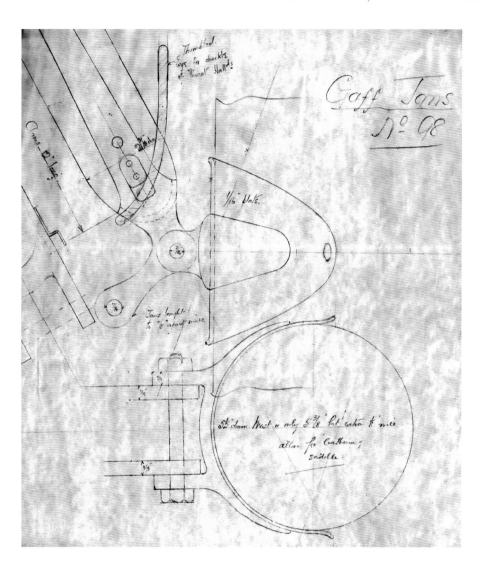

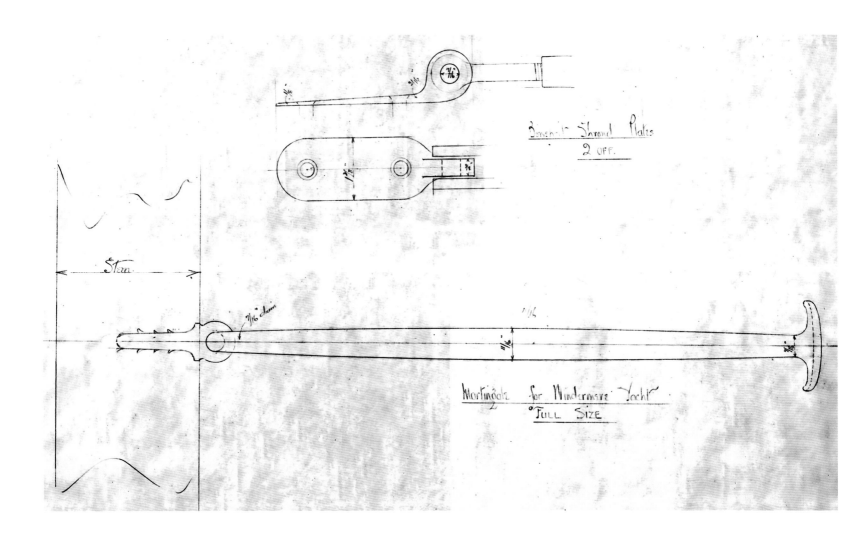

Bronze Shroud Plates
2 OFF.

Stem

7/16" diam

Martingale for Windermere Yacht
FULL SIZE

# CHAPTER 10

*Apache* (later called *Fera*)
Design No. 169
International 6-Metre Class
L.O.A.: 31 ft, ⅜ in.; 9.46 m.
L.W.L.: 20 ft; 6.1 m.
Beam: 6 ft, 1 in.; 1.85 m.
Draft: 3 ft, 11 in.; 1.19 m.
Built by McAlisters, Dumbarton in 1909.

What makes this yacht special is that she was one of the first of the most long-lived successful class of racing yachts. The 'Sixes' still race today, and when they come together for a regatta there are some quite new, and some over ninety years old. They race hard and if the older ones leak a little when robustly driven, at least they only make an acceptable amount of water which the crew can easily manage. When my sister and I had our 'Six', *Finetta*, on one occasion when racing offshore in moderately severe conditions we had to pump thirty minutes every hour. 'Sixes' were not intended for such deep-sea racing, and the low cockpit coamings could not fend off the oncoming waves, which torrented below and filled the cabin almost up to the level of the seats. This level of water is not conducive to winning, so we worked the two pumps a lot and took first prizes, more due to youthful energy than racing skills.

The formula that was used for the Metre classes when they first came out in 1907 was simple and it encouraged boats to be narrow, but not excessively so. It discouraged high freeboard by present-day standards, but these yachts were seaworthy if handled with care, so a few of us raced and cruised them up and down the English Channel and elsewhere in some windy weather, many years ago.

Among the factors that ensured the success of this class was their relative cheapness, at least when the class started. Owners often had new boats built every other year, and a few wealthy yachtsmen ordered a replacement every year, so development was continuous. As always happens, each succeeding generation was longer than the previous one, so the potential top speed was higher. A crew composed entirely of the owner and his amateur friends could win, but it was usual to have a paid hand aboard, and sometimes more than one. These professionals looked after the boats, often in winter as well as summer. On a race day they had the mainsail hoisted ready to leave the mooring promptly when the owner's party arrived, which they often did in the owner's launch. The paid hands were usually employed by a yacht yard or went out fishing commercially all winter. When the weather was fine in the summer they applied yet another coat of varnish on the brightwork, which always included the cockpit coamings, cleats, tiller, seats and so on. The spars and the inside of the boat above the sole were also kept well varnished.

One item in the measurement formula for the Metre classes is the girth, which is the dimension 'round the tummy' of the yacht. Early Metre boats have a well-sloped underside of the keel as seen here, so that the girth measurement is kept small. However, this raises the centre of gravity of the lead ballast, which reduces the stability of the yacht, so she cannot carry as much sail as owners and designers would like. It also results in problems when hauling up and storing the yacht level fore-and-aft. The rule was later changed so that the underside of later yachts have more or less level keel bases.

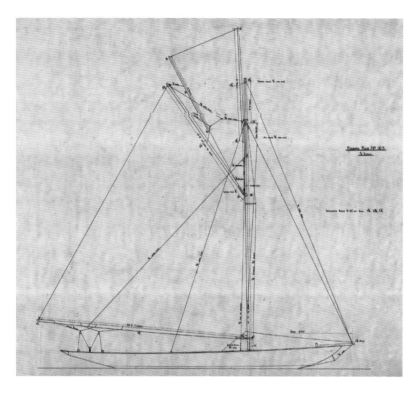

The cockpit of *Apache* is tiny, but there is a hatch amidships that was not hinged but loose. Before a race, this hatch was stored below and one of the crew stood here, spending a lot of his time when on port tack, watching to leeward for starboard tack boats which have right of way. As the class progressed the cockpit became bigger, though a few 'Sixes' had two separate cockpits. A small number of these boats even had three. Designers knew these yachts would be hard driven in rough weather so they wanted plenty of full-width beams to carry the loads. This is one reason for the multiple cockpits. Another was to give the helmsman and crew their own spaces, so that fast working hands and arms would not bump anyone.

When looking at the lines of this yacht, anyone might speculate that she would have carried weather helm because the waterline is so much fuller aft than forward. However, the diagonals, those lines sweeping fore and aft over the topsides in the elevation view, show that the hull is balanced with just a suspicion of more finesse forward as compared with the aft end of the yacht. This aft fullness is a great help when going to windward, and it also helps to coax the buttock lines to run more nearly horizontal. When doing tank tests on a very different design we were fascinated to see how the speed potential increased by just flattening the run up of the buttock lines a little.

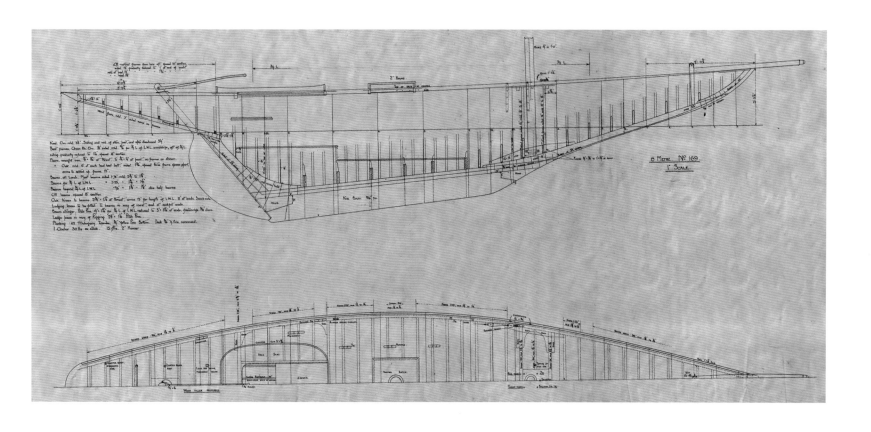

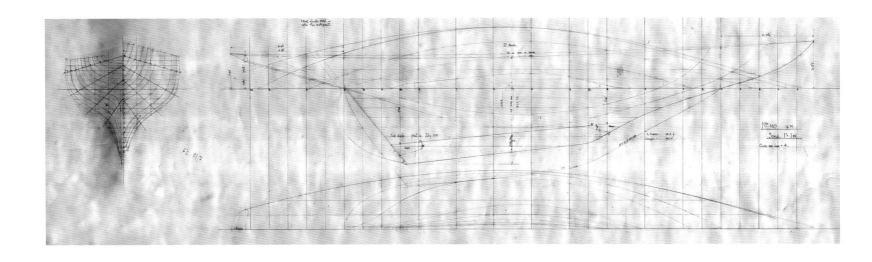

# CHAPTER 11

Dublin Bay 21-Foot Star-Class
Design Nos 80 to 84
L.O.A.: 32 ft, 6 in.; 9.91 m.
L.W.L.: 21 ft; 6.4 m.
Beam: 7 ft, 6 in.; 7.29 m.
Draft: 4 ft, 7 in.; 1.43 m.
Sail area: 630 sq. ft originally; 58.53 sq. m.

This design has all the hallmarks of Alfred Mylne the First. The long overall length when compared with the waterline length, that lovely sweep of stem blending gently into the line along the bottom of the keel and the rake aft of the bottom of the keel are all repeated in other fine designs of his.

In 1911, Alfred Mylne bought Bute Slip Dock on the Isle of Bute with his brother Charles. He worked there a lot, especially every spring when the yachts were being refitted and launched. One thing he would have appreciated was the need to have yachts that were easy to handle ashore. That requires an ample straight length along the bottom of the ballast keel. Boats used to be moved while sitting in cradles that were slid on heavily greased planks. Marine railways were used in those days at almost all the yacht yards for launching and hauling up, so again a straight length of keel base was what every yard manager and foreman

prayed for. Even these days, when so many 'travel-lift' mobile gantries are found, it is a vast help when the bottom of the ballast is straight, because then chocking the boat up for winter storage or repairs is not awkward work.

The construction plan shows unusual features. For instance, the overlap of the stem on the keel is bigger than usual, and then there is a keelson scarphed to the aft end of the stem, with the mast stem spanning the scarph. This makes for a much higher standard of strength than usual, and explains in part why these lovely sleek boats have lasted so well. Anyone building one of these boats today would have a bronze rudder tube instead of the yellow pine that was standard for the class. Yellow pine was also used for the topsides planking, partly because it is light and easily worked. However, from below the turn of the bilge to the keel, the planking is pitch pine. This contains a lot of oil which ensures the wood lasts wonderfully well and explains why the boats of this class have lived so long. Just to emphasise what well thought-out boats these are, the top plank is teak, the king of woods and among those which last longest.

One of the few concessions to saving money was the use of galvanised screws to hold the beam ends. It is irritating the way the galvanising lasts for years if done properly by the 'hot dip' process, then starts to fail and allows rust to grow and grow. The cabin coamings are vertical because this is logical and the cheapest way to build. When yachts were being built of wood in the 1950s and 1960s, builders would charge extra if an owner wanted cabin coamings tilted inboard at the top for a streamlined effect and modern appearance.

This is a true racing yacht, so the small sleek cabin top stops aft of the mast, giving the crew an uncluttered walking and working space round the mast and all over the foredeck. The cabin was deliberately made stark because the principle activity of this class was afternoon

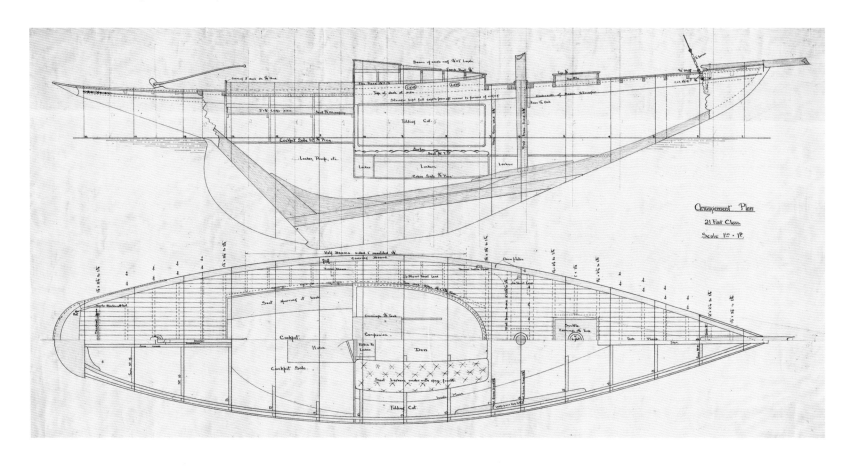

racing. Anyone who wanted to cruise for a weekend had just enough space for two hardy sailors, but three would be a crowd for many people. However, sailing families of two adults and two children have often cruised in boats this size and had enormous fun. Some of this class are still sailing today, proof that good design and construction lasts and lasts.

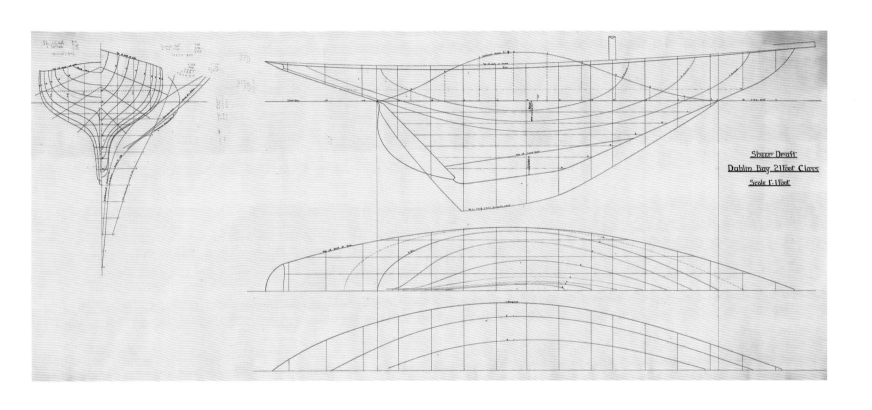

Sheer Draft
Dublin Bay 21 Foot Class
Scale 1": 1 Foot

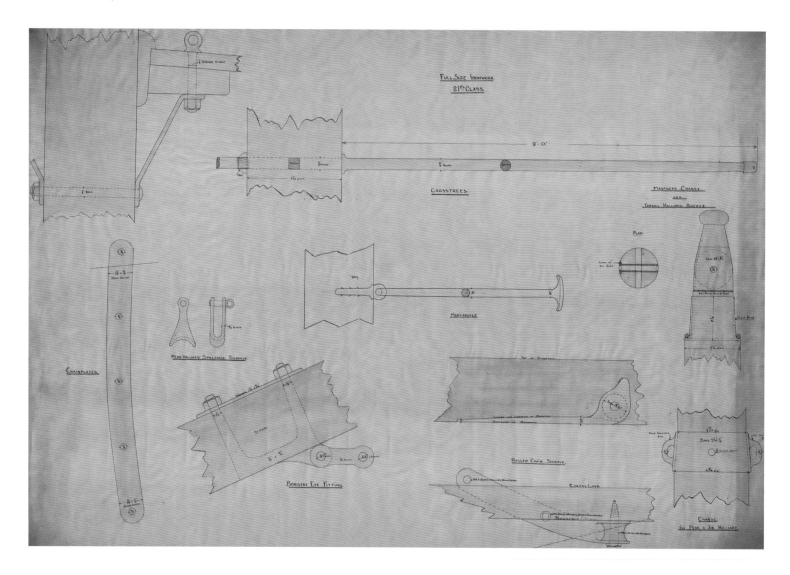

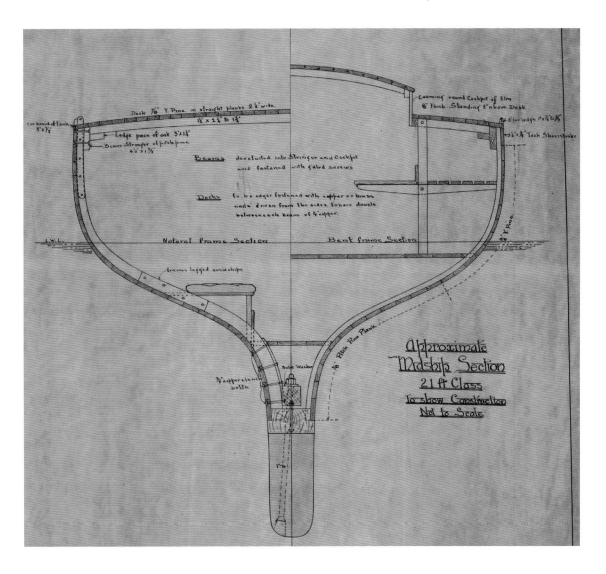

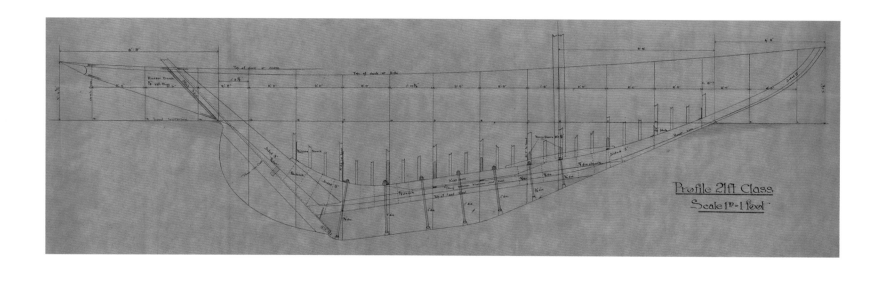

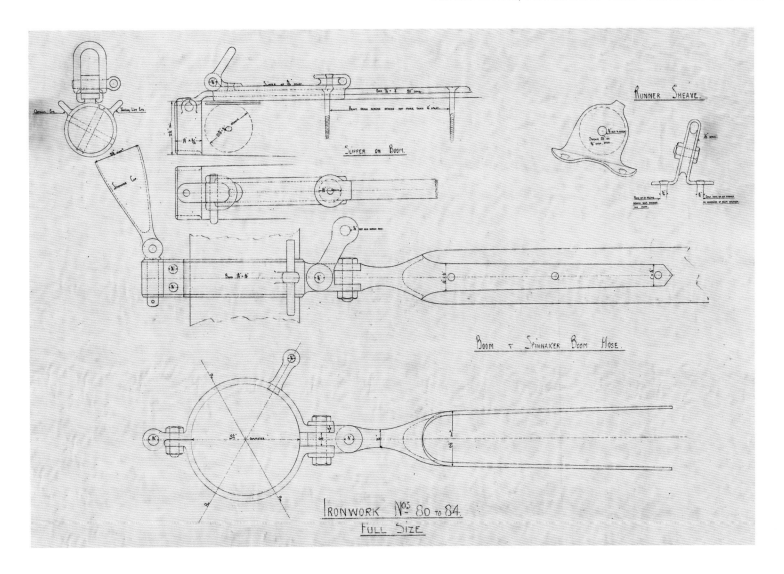

RUNNER SHEAVE.

SLIPPER ON BOOM.

BOOM & SPINNAKER BOOM HOSE.

IRONWORK Nos 80 to 84.
FULL SIZE

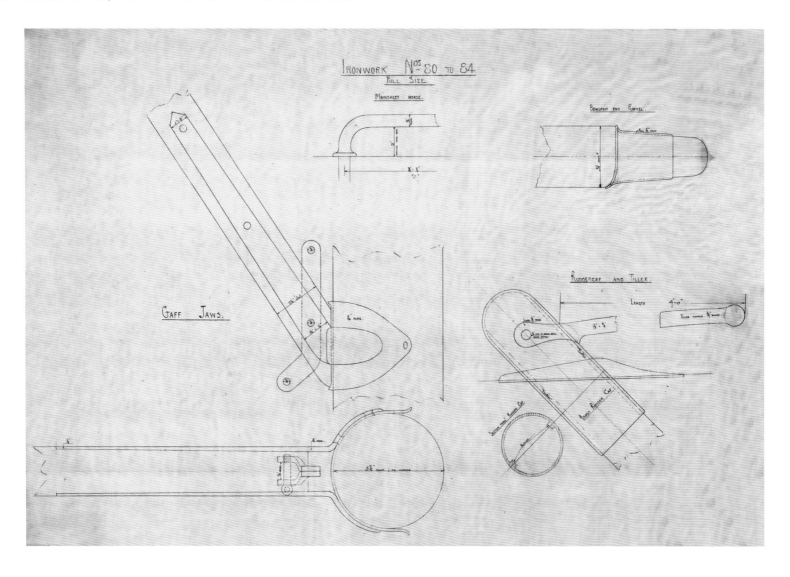

# CHAPTER 12

Royal North Of Ireland Yacht Club Island-Class

Design No. 193

L.O.A.: 39 ft, 5 in.; 12.01 m.

L.W.L.: 27 ft; 8.23 m.

Beam: 9 ft, 2 in.; 2.79 m.

Draft: 5 ft, 7 in.; 1.70 m.

Sail Area: originally 995 sq. ft; 92. 44 sq. m. Later, typically 684 sq. ft; 63. 54 sq. m.

The essence of a One Design class is that all the yachts in it must be identical. This ensures that the best helmsman wins the races, provided he is backed up by a good crew. A principle reason for buying a One Design yacht is that it will be cheaper than other craft of the same size, because there can be at least some degree of mass production during the building. For instance, the shadow sections round which the hull is build are only made once, but used for all the yachts in the class. Also, the planking, frames, beams etc. for several yachts can be made in the sawmill all at the same time. This speeds up production and reduces costs.

When designing this class, there are subtle signs that Alfred Mylne was going for simplicity, a fair measure of comfort and an affordable price. For instance, there is just a single headsail and this jib is small as it does not overlap the mast. Also, it is set on a relatively short bowsprit, this sprit itself being an inexpensive spar due to its limited length. A sensible detail is the split topping lift on the mizzen mast to help the sail to stay under control when it is being hoisted or dropped. This is important as more than half of this sail is aft of the end of the counter.

The lines plan shows a fast hull shape, but there are subtle indications that speed is not the only consideration. The underside of the counter runs up at about 18.5 degrees to the horizontal, suggesting that Alfred Mylne was keen to make the cabin roomy and comfortable. The shallow cockpit is unusual for this vintage of yacht, and anyone who has cruised in the Irish Sea will appreciate that it makes sense to have a cockpit well which cannot flood into the cabin, or contain so much water that the freeboard aft is dangerously reduced in severe weather.

This class has been so successful that several boats are still around, giving pleasure to their owners and crew. These yachts reconfirm that a pretty, well-designed and well-built yacht lasts a long time. What a contrast this is to cars that seldom last twenty years and many are 'dead' after ten years. Looking at the lovely sweep of the sheer – the line of the deck in elevation – it is clear that these boats were designed and built to be beautiful: to inspire love and affection; to teach successive generations about the bliss of going afloat; to experience the friendliness of sailing; to feel the excitement of danger when the wind blasts over the water and to know the solid pleasure of beating the elements and reaching harbour safely. What sport can begin to compare with sailing and racing for people of all ages?

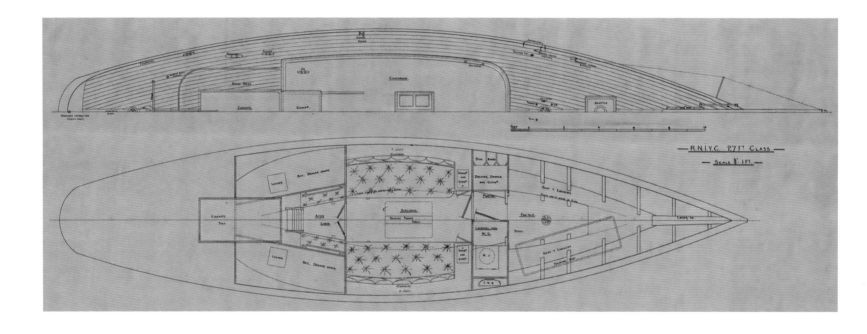

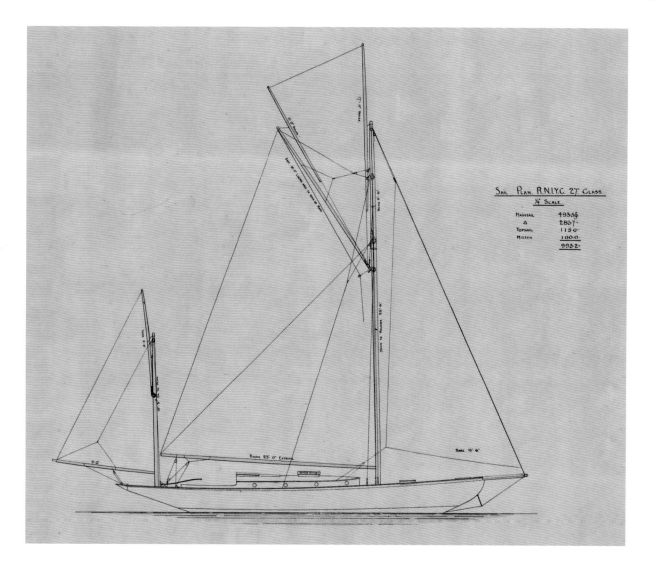

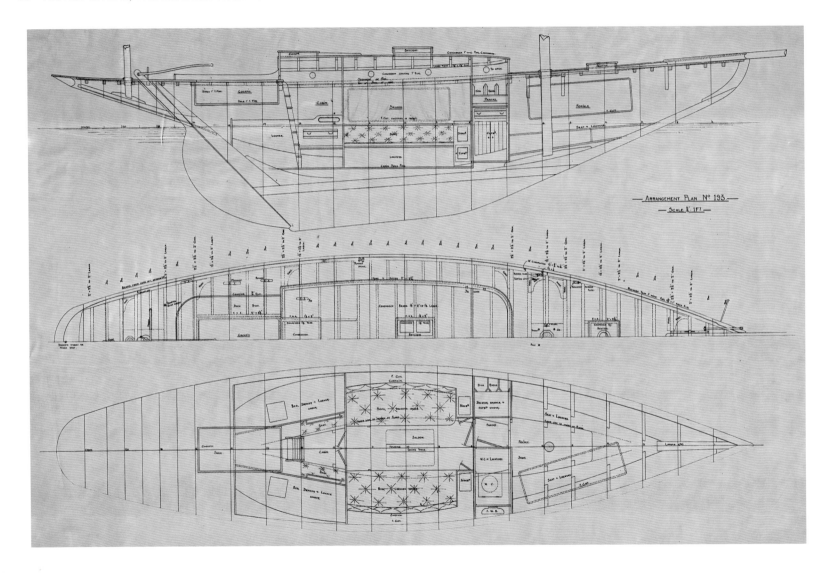

ARRANGEMENT PLAN No 193
SCALE ⅜" 1FT

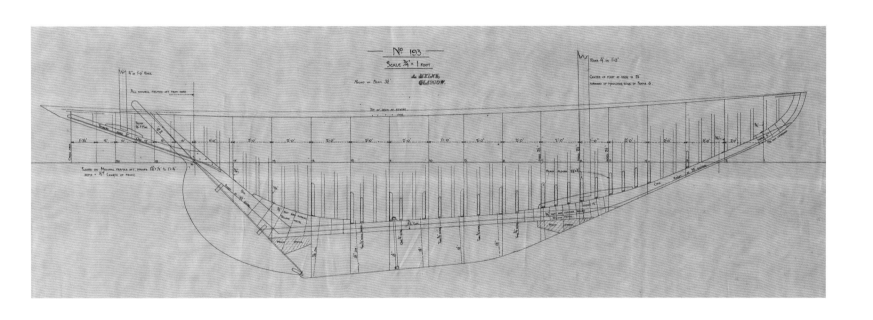

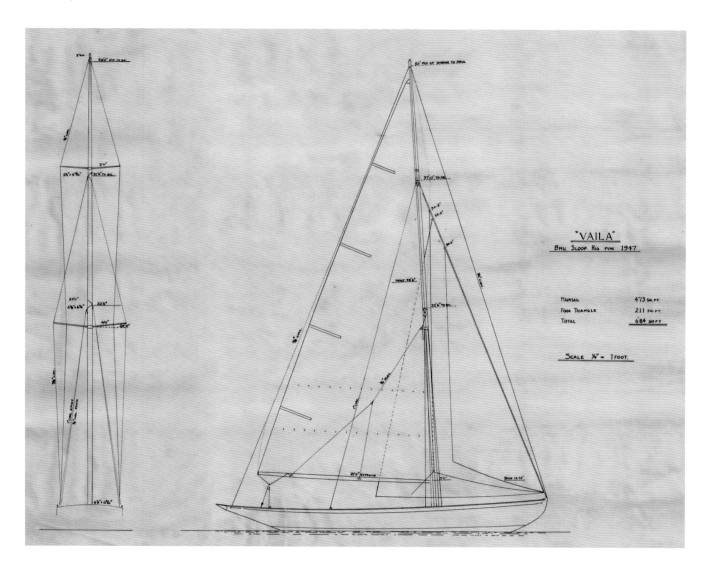

# CHAPTER 13

*Sentinel*
Design No. 55
Length overall: 40 ft; 12.19 m.
Length waterline: 28 ft; 8.534 m.
Beam: 10 ft, 6 in.; 3.20 m.
Draft: 3 ft, 10 in. and 7 ft, 8 in.; 1.170 m and 2.320 m.
Sail area: 933 sq. ft; 86.68 sq. m.
Built by W. Wilson, Annan, in 1900.

Annan, where this yacht was built, is on the Solway Firth in western Scotland. This is a wide and shallow estuary with several small rivers running into it. In the pre-First World War days, seabirds of every sort were numerous and a few men made their living shooting them. Men of means took to the sport and some had shallow-draft yachts specially built for duck shooting. It seems highly likely that *Sentinel* was first owned by someone who enjoyed this game. The large solid fuel stove, with its chimney extending up through the deck, would have kept the whole boat wonderfully warm in the coldest winter when the shooting was at its best.

Any boat operating in shallow waters is bound to go aground often, which explains in part why this yacht has such a gently rounded shape at the toe of the keel. If she was going slowly when she grounded the crew would hardly notice and would often be able to pole her into deep water without too much of a struggle. Thanks to her shallow draft, they could hop over the side and shove her back into deeper water if they were athletic and not afraid of getting wet.

When the centreboard is right down the draft is doubled, and experienced seamen used to use the centreboard as a 'sounding lead' in the days before echo sounders became cheap and popular after the Second World War. This centreboard is made of ¾-inch (20 mm) galvanised plate, so it would hardly ever come to any harm if it was left down as the yacht entered shoal waters. When the board was heard rumbling along the seabed it would be hoisted up a little and the yacht put about into deeper water. Some yachtsmen still use this technique, as it tends to be more precisely accurate than even the best echo-sounder, and it is more exciting, working to the nearest thumb thickness.

The centreboard is hoisted by a tackle, which is secured to the foot of the mast and made fast onto a cleat on top of the fore-end of the centreboard case. This is not a convenient arrangement and later yachts have the hoist led up and back to the fore-end of the cockpit. The design of the centreboard is less than perfect, in that there is no chock or device to prevent it dropping right down if the tackle breaks or wears out.

As originally designed, this yacht had a single headsail with a boom along the foot so that it was self-tacking. It was cut low and in bad weather might have been scary if it collected a succession of waves breaking inboard. The final sail plan shows a fore triangle base extended from 17 feet to 18 feet 10 inches (5.18 to 5.74 m) by moving the mast back, and providing a staysail and jib. The topsail's jackyard, or forward spar, was designed with a slight curve aft, but in the final sail plan this spar is more traditional and straight. Curved spars are something designers love to draw, but many builders dislike making them because of the complications and the chances of getting the curve wrong. For this sort of work an average level of skill is not enough.

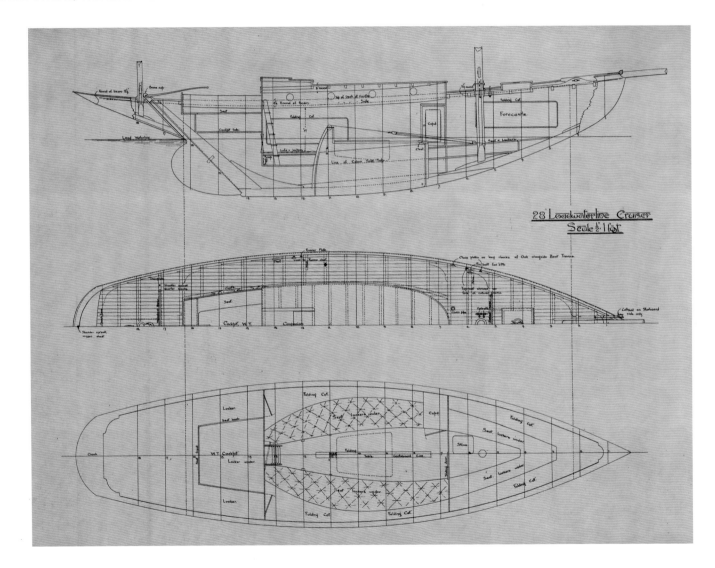

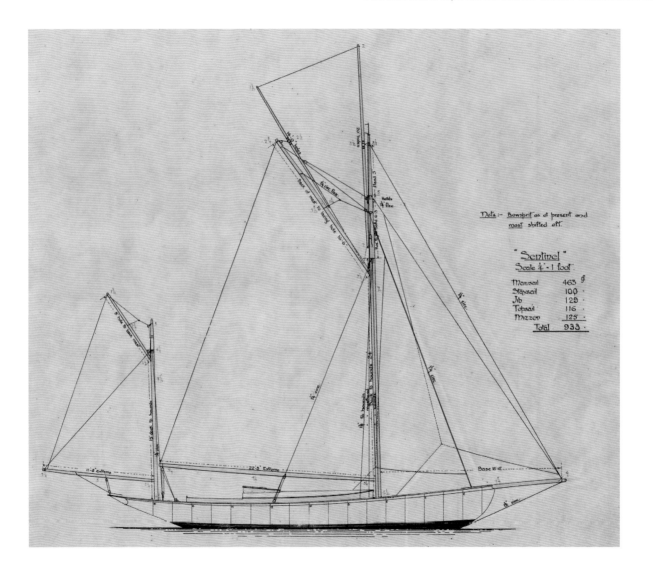

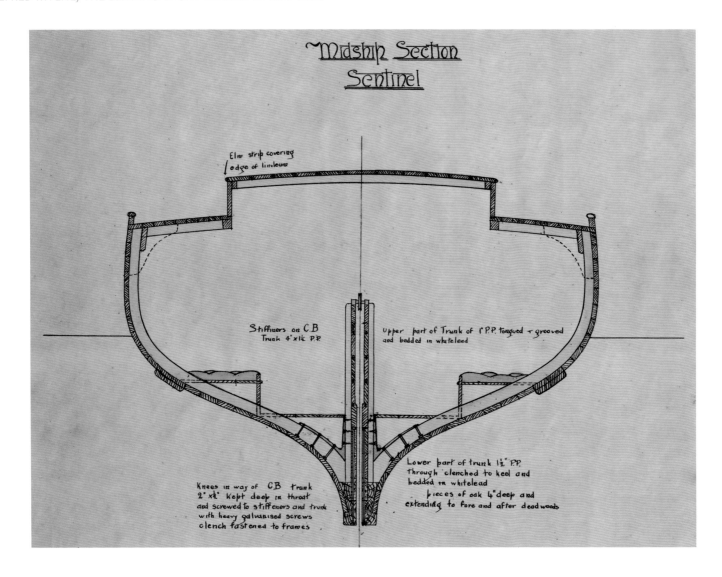

Midship Section
Sentinel

Elm strip covering edge of linoleum

Stiffeners on C.B
Trunk 4"x1½" P.P.

Upper part of Trunk of 1" P.P. tongued & grooved
and bedded in whitelead

Knees in way of CB trunk
2"x¾" kept deep in throat
and screwed to stiffeners and trunk
with heavy galvanised screws
clench fastened to frames

Lower part of trunk 1½" P.P.
through clenched to keel and
bedded in whitelead
pieces of oak 4" deep and
extending to fore and after deadwoods

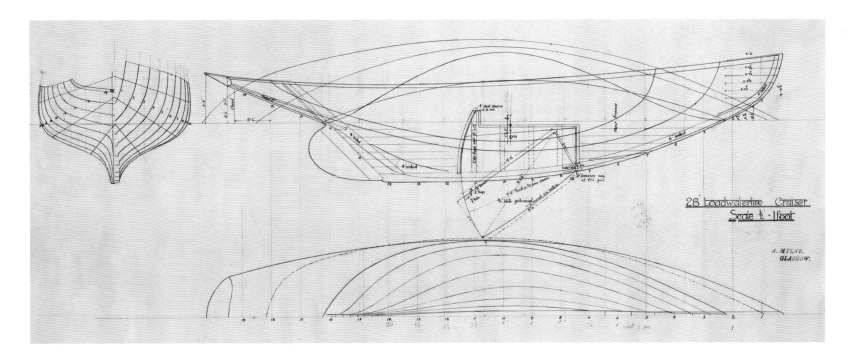

When this yacht was built she was given a watertight cockpit, which was unusual then. One reason why everyone wants a self-drainer is to deal with rain-water that comes aboard during the week when the boat is unattended. But when this yacht was built many moorings had a boatman who went round and for a small fee kept all the yachts under his care regularly pumped out. These useful fellows would also dry the sails, and this was an extremely important job in the days when sails were made of cotton and prone to rotting soon, fast and often. After a wet weekend many owners would leave wet sails bundled loosely in the cabins, returning the next weekend to be greeted by a fusty, pungent odour and everything on board wet with condensation. Yachtsmen and women were so much tougher in those days.

# CHAPTER 14

*Vladimir* (later *Medea*) Clyde 30-Foot-Class
Design No. 106
L.O.A.: 40 ft, 6 in.; 12.34 m.
L.W.L.: 26 ft, 6 in.; 8.08 m.
Beam: 8 ft, 2 in.; 2.49 m.
Draft: 6 ft, 2 in.; 1.88 m.
Sail Area: originally 995 sq. ft; 92.44 sq. m.
Built by Robertsons, Sandbank in 1904.

In several respects this is one of the most interesting yachts in this book. She was for many decades owned by Alfred Myle the First. When he died his widow kept the yacht, but it was maintained and used by Alfred Mylne the Second, nephew of the First. The two Mylnes cruised and raced this yacht under the name *Medea* with success on the Clyde long after many yachts built around the same time had been broken up because they were no longer seaworthy.

The Clyde 30-Foot Class was not large and when the International Metre Rule came into force in 1907, the 'Thirties' raced with the new International 8 Metre Class.

Alfred Mylne the First was offered this yacht at a low price because she was widely believed to be out-classed. When he bought her, an old International 6-Metre yacht was 'thrown in' as part of the purchase, much as these days there is often a dinghy with a yacht being sold. As was the custom, the old out-classed 'Six' was broken up and her lead keel melted down for a new racing yacht being built at the Mylne yacht yard, Bute Slip Dock at Ardmaleish, on the Isle of Bute.

Both Mylnes cruised this yacht more or less single-handedly because they were accomplished seamen. Each Mylne was often crewed by his wife, but these ladies were not always excited by the prospect, because, with her low freeboard, *Medea* was a wet boat, and facilities on board were limited. None of that generation of cruisers had running cold or hot water or showers on board. Through each summer, apart from the war years, the Mylnes raced in local handicap events organised by the clubs in the area. These included the Royal Northern Y.C., the Royal Clyde Y.C., the Royal Western Y.C., the Mudhook Y.C., the Clyde Corinthian Y.C and the Clyde Cruising Club.

The original gaff sail plan gave way to a modern Bermudan one, with the area cut down first to 820 sq. feet (76.18 sq. metres) and later to 680 sq. feet (63.17 sq. metres). This was mainly for easier handling but also to reduce the loadings on the aging hull so as to minimise leaking when hard driven in a tough race. Few yachts can have a racing history spanning sixty years, as this one did. She would probably be sailing still if she had not suffered from a broken mooring near Dublin, which resulted in her going ashore on a rocky beach and becoming a total wreck. An important reason why this lovely sleek hull lasted so long is because the bottom planking was of pitch pine, which contains resin which resists rot. The topsides were cedar, also a wood which has an oily compound in it. But a truly remarkable thing is that the bottom planking was only 1 inch, or 25 mm, thick and the topsides planking only ⅞ inch, or 22 mm, thick.

When Alfred Mylne the First owned *Medea* he liked to get right away for a holiday, free from everyday worries. To this end he used to sail to the very top of Loch Fyne and anchor there, where, today, even though there are a hundred times more yachts on the West Coast of Scotland, this is still a secluded spot, rarely visited by any craft. In the days when there were no mobile phones or VHF radios, Mylne could be sure no-one would be able to contact him till he sailed back to his moorings and went ashore.

Like all the best designers, Alfred Mylne was constantly innovating, but he realised that some ideas should first be tested on his own yacht before recommending them for clients' craft. When crewed only by his wife, he needed an easily handled sail plan, and he sometimes used a jib hanked onto mast slides instead of a full-sized mainsail. This was in effect a trisail for use in rough but not extreme weather.

When Alfred Mylne the Second took over this lovely boat he regularly made changes so that she was more comfortable for his family, which included a son and daughter. After 1945, there was a general move towards standing masts on cabin tops to reduce the loading on the stem-to-keel join and the garboard planks that so often leaked. Comfort on board was enhanced by having two under-deck supporting pillars forming a good-sized doorway where formerly there was the mast. Originally, anyone wanting to go forward from the saloon had to struggle round the large wood mast which occupied the centre of the passageway. A whole new cabin top, complete with long elegant doghouse, made the cabin larger with much better headroom and ample daylight. At the fore-end of the new cabin top there was a fore hatch, well above the fore-deck and therefore less likely to leak when beating to windward in tough conditions. The new arrangement gave moderate headroom in the fore cabin. On deck stanchions and lifelines were added as well as a pulpit.

The design of this yacht proves, yet again, that a well-built racing boat can have a long second life as a cruiser, which can also do well in club races all the world over. When the wonderfully successful International Metre Rule was launched in 1907 a major innovation was the fact

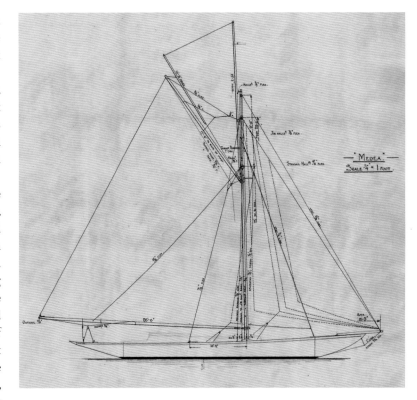

that all yachts built to this new Rule had to be constructed to Lloyds' scantlings. As a result, the frames for the most part have metal floors at the bottom, adding massive strength where is needed. In contrast *Medea*, ex-*Vladimir*, only has them from a little forward of the mast to a short distance aft of amidships because she was not built as a Metre-class yacht but as a 'Clyde Thirty-Footer'.

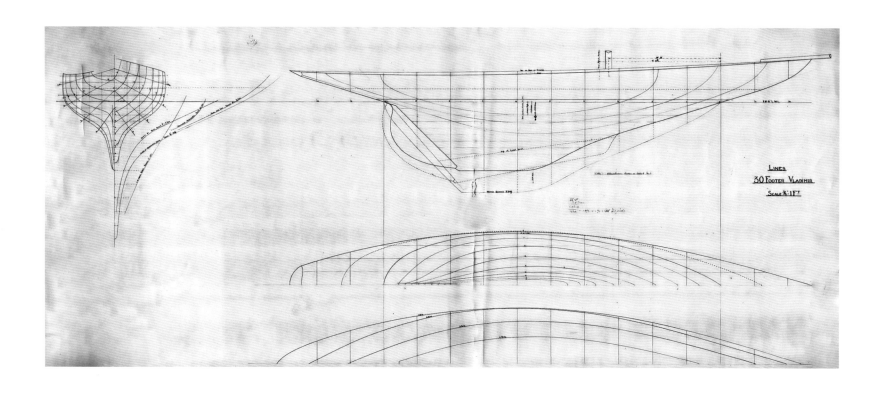

LINES
30 FOOTER VLADIMIR
SCALE ¾:1 FT

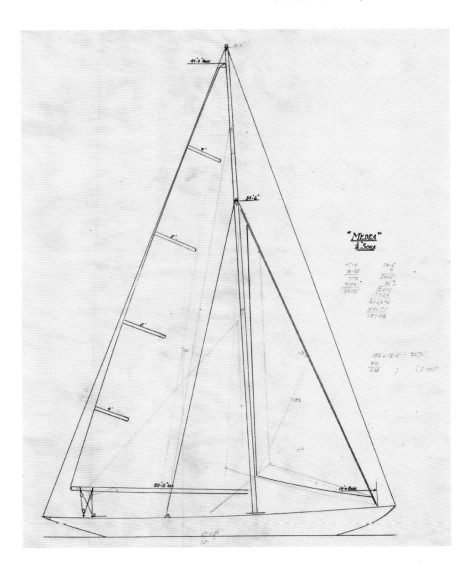

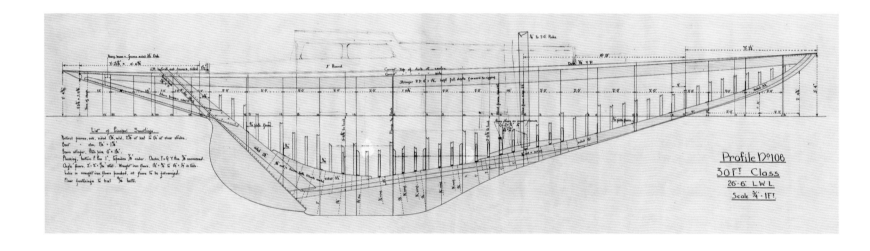

# CHAPTER 15

*Aline*
Design No. 167
L.O.A.: 42 ft, 4 in.; 12.90 m.
L.W.L.: 27 ft; 8.23 m.
Beam: 8 ft, 8 in.; 2.64 m.
Draft: 5 ft, 9 in.; 1.75 m.
Sail Area: 1078 sq. ft; 100.15 sq. m.
Built in 1909 by A. Malcolm, Port Bannatine.

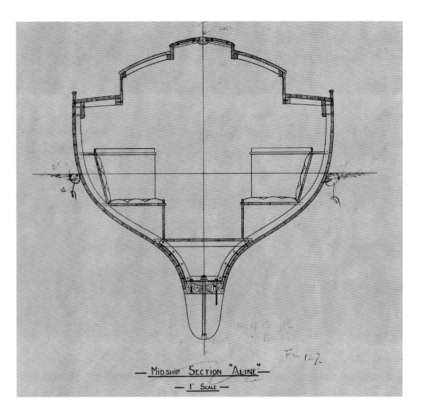

— MIDSHIP SECTION "ALINE" —
— 1" SCALE —

With almost the same overall length as and a roughly comparable waterline length to the Clyde 30-Foot Class racing yacht in the previous chapter, this cruiser is different. With 15 inches, or 375 mm, more beam, as well as a neat low cabin top, there is a lot more room and comfort inside. She was just as strongly built as the previous yacht, and to prove it she was racing long after the end of the Second World War. In 1937 she beat all comers in the Clyde Cruising Club race to Tarbert on Loch Fyne, and she had a habit of slipping along faster than many younger craft, year after year. She stayed on the Clyde where she had the reputation of being one of the fastest, loveliest boats afloat.

The original gaff sail plan, with runners to the masthead and to the hounds, as well as two sets of headsail sheets, must have made for exciting tacking in rough conditions. The work involved would have been enough to raise a sweat as the headsail sheets were merely doubled to give a two-to-one purchase. This would have been too little for the average amateur, whose city-softened hands would soon have blistered in a long tough beat. Gloves for sailing are a fairly recent invention. Fitted in 1937, the Bermudan rig was far easier to handle with no runners, a permanent backstay, which needed no tending except by a keen racing crew who would have adjusted it off the wind, and the headsail sheets were hauled in using sheet winches. *Aline* was just one of the many yachts which had their gaff rigs changed to Bermudan between 1920 and 1939. After the Second World War, very few new yachts came out with gaff rigs and most of the yachts built before that war that originally had a gaff rig were changed to the taller rig, mainly because it was more efficient to windward. It was also easier to set and handle.

During the era of the big rig change, two major advantages were always quoted in favour of the Bermudan arrangement. The first was the removal of the bowsprit, which many people hated because when changing sails in heavy weather, someone had to climb out to the front of this spar. This usually meant getting saturated, and sometimes totally dunked. It was quite common to wear ordinary wellington boots in severe weather, and these got filled with water even in quite mild conditions. This generation of yachts did not have high topsides so their bowsprits were low down near the sea – and below it if the boat was pitching.

A second big advantage of the high Bermudan rig was the matching shorter boom. When reefing these were far easier to handle, especially when the aft end of the boom was well forward of the counter end, as on *Aline*.

Like so many yachts of her era, there were various changes to the accommodation. The original layout was designed for an owner and friend, while most of the work would have been done by the two paid hands who lived in the for'c'sle. Later, a quarter berth was worked in on the starboard side. Also, a passage berth took over the space originally occupied by the port forward sideboard in the saloon and the pantry, which today we would call the galley. These two changes are seen pencilled in on the cabin layout plan. The original two-primus stove cooker was on the starboard side just aft of the mast.

When this yacht was built it was rare for an engine to be fitted. Thirty years later it was unusual for a cruiser to be launched without an engine, though the petrol engines widely used were often not reliable, and were tiny by today's standards. An engine was fitted in this yacht, and the technique used was one developed for fishing boats which were originally sail-powered but later had an engine put in. To avoid the expense and potential damage caused by drilling through the stern post, the propeller was brought out to one side, ahead of and clear of the rudder. This tended to result in a boat that turned one way better than the other, but this attribute could be used to advantage getting out of a cramped harbour by skilful seamanship.

The midship construction section shows how *Aline* was built. The extra strong beams, one forward and one aft of the mast, extend right across the yacht, forward of the cabin top, so that this area where there are mast stresses is extra rugged. Steel angle bar floors extend up to sole level and are shown with four bolts in each arm. *Aline* had high toe-rails, which in a small way compensated for the absence of stanchions and guard-rails wires that came into common use after 1920. Before that crews held on tight, and sometimes fell overboard. The toe-rail is shown with the traditional 'bottle-top' capping, which looks something like a champagne cork with its top gently sloping downwards in an elegant subtle curve on the inboard and outboard sides. This section shape is expensive to make. As a result, it is seldom seen these days, when the 'money-men' dominate yacht production and quality takes second, or twenty-second, place in the order of priorities. Few people in the yacht industry, apart from the oldest and best taught, know that the 'bottle-top' design makes a great deal of sense. Its shape sheds rain and spray that helps to preserve the varnish, but, above all, it looks so much better than a flat, boring, top surface.

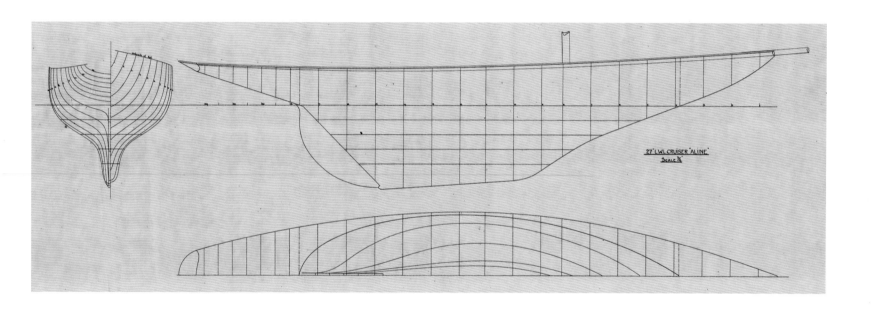

27'LWL CRUISER 'ALINE'
Scale ⅜"

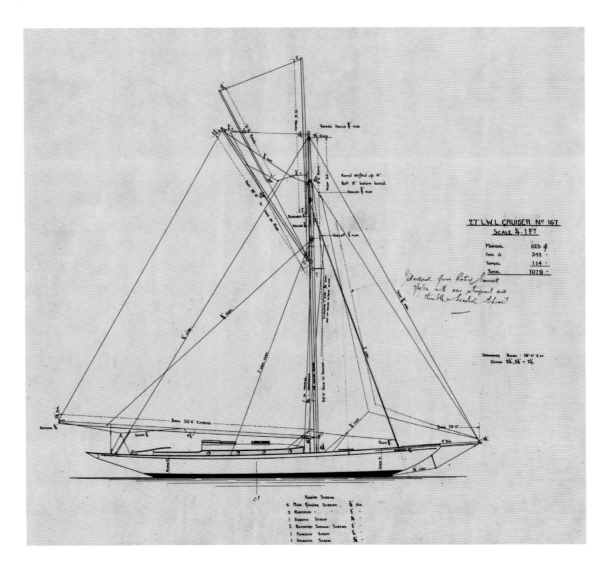

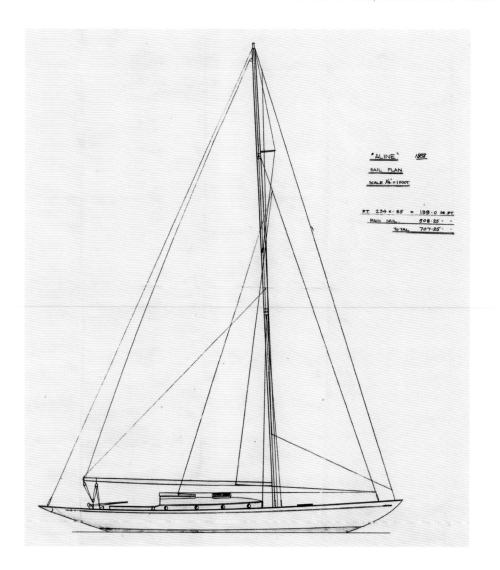

"ALINE"   1888

SAIL   PLAN

SCALE ⅛" = 1 FOOT

P.T.  234 × .85  =  199.0 SQ. FT
MAIN SAIL.              508.25   "
            TOTAL     707.25   "

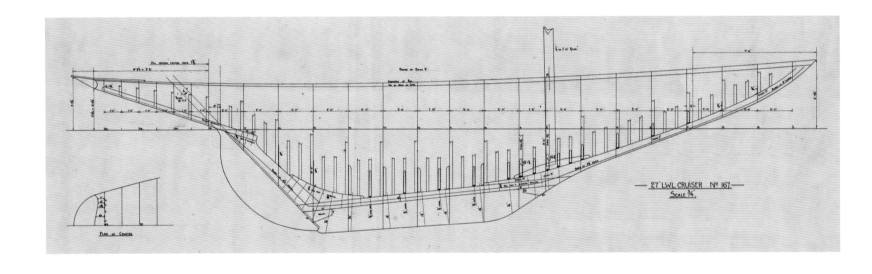

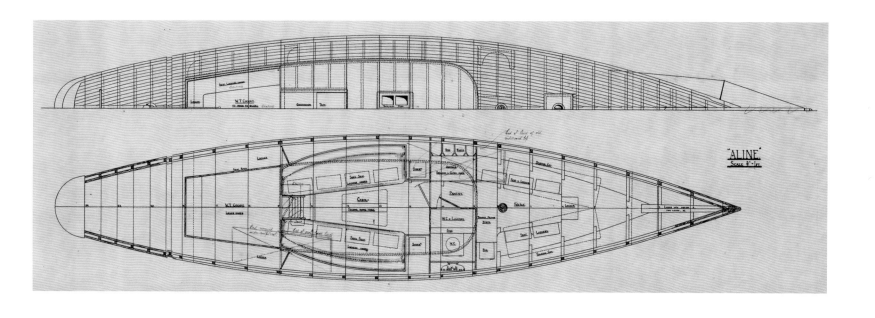

# CHAPTER 16

Clyde One Design Class
Design No. 41
Length overall: 50 ft; 15.24 m.
Length waterline: 35 ft; 10.668 m.
Beam: 11 ft; 3.353 m.
Draft: 8 ft; 2.438 m.
Sail areas: 1715 sq. ft; 159.32 sq. m nominal, including mainsail, fore triangle and topsail
Built in 1899.

The design of a yacht is a balancing act, compared with which walking a tight-rope is as easy as falling off a log. A good example of this need to assess advantages and disadvantages at every stage in the design is seen in the bottom of the ballast keel, which is a straight horizontal line. Every designer of this general type of yacht has a problem getting the fore-end of the ballast keel as low as possible to give good stability, so a horizontal line makes eminent sense. However, if the yacht is trimmed down by the bow, then what was a horizontal line now dips down at the fore-end. This can result in a low pressure area along the bottom of the keel and steering problems may occur in windy weather.

There's more. When running fast downwind, a wave may lift the stern, so the underside of the keel becomes higher at the aft end, just when

reliable positive steering is urgently needed. If the underside of the keel was flat, as it is in many designs when the aim is to get as much metal ballast as low as possible, this aft upward slope can be a worry. However, all the sections in this design are fully-rounded keel, so the chances of negative pressure on the aft end of the keel base are reduced, probably to near zero.

Most Mylne designs have the fore-end of the keel base higher than the aft end in what might be described as the conventional way. One subsidiary reason is that slipping a boat on a marine railway is simpler and safer with that shape. By 1911, when Mylne owned the small boatyard called Bute Slip Dock with his brother, he would want every yacht to be easy to bring ashore on the marine railway.

The load waterline is far fuller aft than forward, as in virtually all fast boats. This is partly because the bow sections have to fight through the waves, so the finer they are, the less water has to be shouldered aside. Just as important, the yacht must have a tendency to surge to windward as she heels, and the full aft sections ensure this happens because the stern is raised relative to the bow. This counteracts the negative or downward pull of the water flow as it accelerates up the stern.

The original sail plan was typical of its time, with three small headsails. The three paid hands would not have too much trouble sheeting these in at each tack, as the staysail and lower jib sheets were through blocks, giving a two-to-one purchase. There were no sheet winches when this class was started. It was not until the 1930s, when large overlapping headsails became all the rage, that sheet winches became common and indeed essential.

Some of the real excitement when tacking this style of yacht is at the runners, especially the topmast set. They each have tackles, but getting from port to starboard under the boom and clear of the main sheet calls for special agility. In practice, the two leeward runners would usually be let off by one person, and the windward two set up by two others. The amateurs in the crew often did these jobs.

The most awkward part of tacking would be getting the jib topsail from side to side round the luff of the staysail. Plenty of people would let the wind in the sail force it across onto the new side once the bow was through the wind. This is fine for cruising but not the most efficient way to tack when racing.

With seven halyards and a topping lift, also a jackyard topsail downhaul, there were a lot of ropes coming down to deck level. To deal with them there were pinrails port and starboard just inboard of the chain plates. These handy securing points are now only seen on a few traditional craft, so their advantages and problems are seldom appreciated. One reason seamen liked them was the speed with which a halyard could be let go. Once it was hauled right up, the rope was taken under the bottom of the pin, round the top, and back down and under several times. However, to free off the halyard it was not necessary to reverse the process, one just yanked the pin upwards and the rope was freed in an instant. This is so handy when the topsail had to be dropped swiftly in a squall.

The 1930 sail plan is vastly simpler and would cost a lot less to maintain. The boat would be slower under many conditions, especially downwind and reaching in light conditions, because the total area is reduced to 59 per cent of the original generous acreage. However, there is only one set of runners and the headsail is self-tacking with an unusual boom that does not extend the full length of the foot. This arrangement is handy when lowering the sail as the boom lands on the deck with the sail on top of it, so a few sail tyers round the lot keeps the sail quiescent while the mooring is sorted out, or the anchor lowered.

This sort of boom needs a set of alternative securing points for the sheet to get the best from the sail. Going onto the fore-deck when

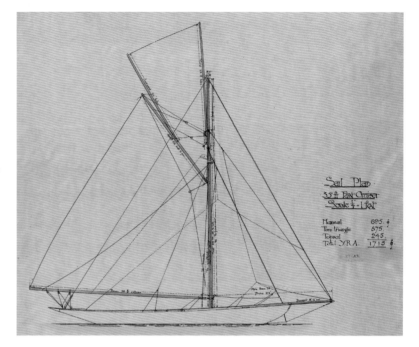

the sail is thrashing back and forth is not advisable, and a good case can be made for having a downhaul secured to the top jib hank so that the sail is quickly forced down onto the deck. Now that so many modern boats have roller furling headsails this type of down-haul is rarely seen, but it can be a considerable asset when cruising with a hanked on headsail.

The single crosstree, with shrouds at the outer ends and intermediate shrouds about one third of the length of the crosstree inboard, was popular at the time because it cuts down windage aloft and is simple, so it saves money. However, it is not truly efficient at keeping the mast straight. Also, when lying alongside other yachts, the way the crosstrees extend so far outboard of the hull is a menace. If there are power boats passing and causing the yacht to pitch up and down, the crosstrees of adjacent yachts clash.

The midship construction section makes it clear the yachts in this class were designed for speed. The lower planking was pitch pine, and this explains in part why some yachts in this class have lasted so long, because the pitch in the wood excludes water and helps to keep rot at bay. The upper planks were yellow pine, 1 ⅛ inches, or 28.6 mm, thick. However, the lower planks were 1 ¼ inches thick, so in theory there would be a little 'step' ⅛ inch, or 3 mm, high between the two different woods. In practice, when the yacht was planked the shipwrights faired off the planking by planing it all over. They would skim off the 'step' as they worked their way all over the hull, ensuring the finished boat would have a faultlessly smooth appearance.

Anyone who has used a large plane on a vertical surface for half an hour will know it is brutally hard work. The shipwrights who built these boats kept at it all day, and once they had cleaned off the surface down to the waterline they were working under the turn of the bilge. This was overhead planing, a much tougher job. But then they were hardy men who worked long hours, often in bad conditions. Building sheds were seldom heated and the staging they stood on was often less than rigid, making the job even tougher.

The cabin sole was supported by 2 × 2 ¼ inch, or 50 × 56 mm, larch, called beams on the construction plan. This shows that Mylne was keen to work in strength low down because he knew that these boats would be raced hard. The flush deck, with its small hatches and skylights, ensures there are plenty of full-width beams throughout the length of the boat, apart from in way of the cockpit.

Between the cockpit and the companionway there is a bridge deck with a strong beam, so the deck is well supported throughout its length, and the two sides of the yacht strongly gripped together. When looking at some modern yachts with large cabin top windows and hatches close to the mast, just where the stresses are high, it is clear that some designers' work has been sabotaged by stylists. Such an arrangement cannot be sensible or seaworthy, and indicates that the vessel will probably not have a long life, especially if she is driven hard offshore.

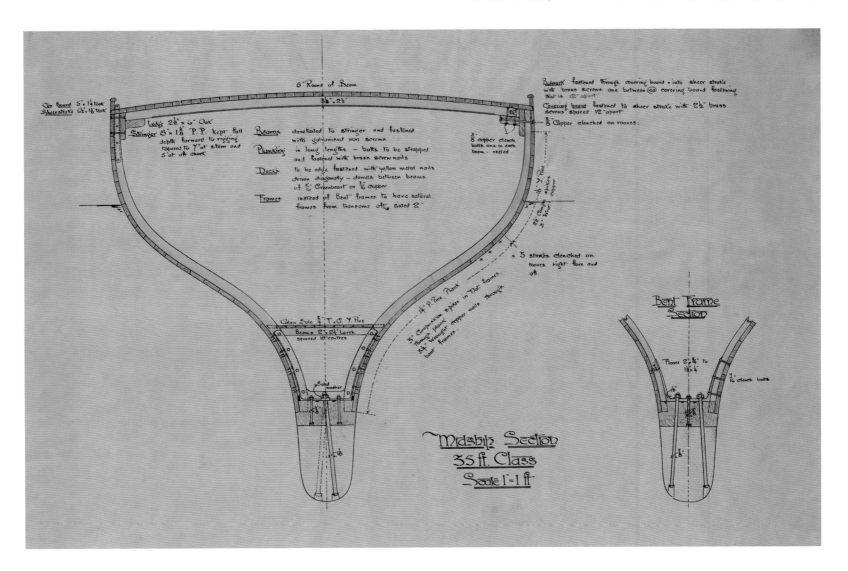

5" Round of Beam.

$3\frac{1}{2}$" × $2\frac{1}{2}$"

Cov. Board 5" × 1$\frac{1}{4}$" teak
Sheerstrake 6$\frac{1}{2}$" 1$\frac{1}{2}$" teak

Ledge 2$\frac{1}{2}$" × 6" Oak.

Stringer 8" × 1$\frac{5}{8}$" P.P. kept full depth forward to rigging tapered to Y" at stem and 5" at aft chock.

Beams    dovetailed to stringer and fastened with galvanised iron screws.

Planking  in long lengths — butts to be strapped and fastened with brass screw nails.

Decks    to be edge fastened with yellow metal nails driven diagonally — dowels between beams of $\frac{5}{16}$" Greenheart or $\frac{3}{16}$" copper.

Frames   instead of Bent frames to have natural frames from transome aft, sided 2".

Bulwark fastened through covering board + into sheer strake with brass screws one between e@ covering board fastening that is 12" apart.

Covering board fastened to sheer strake with 2$\frac{1}{2}$" brass screws spaced 12" apart.

$\frac{3}{8}$" Copper clenched on rooves.

$\frac{3}{8}$" copper clench bolts one in each beam - reeled.

16" Y Pine.

$2\frac{1}{2}$" Clench nails $\frac{3}{16}$" copper.

3 strakes clenched on rooves right fore and aft.

4" P. Pine. Plank.

3" Composition spikes in Nat. frames through plank

3$\frac{1}{2}$" " " copper nails through bent frames.

Cabin Sole $\frac{5}{8}$" T. & Y. Pine

Beams 2" × 2$\frac{1}{2}$" Larch.
spaced 18" centres.

Solid washer.

Midship Section
35 ft. Class
Scale 1" = 1 ft

Bent Frame Section

Floors 2" 2$\frac{1}{2}$" to 1$\frac{1}{2}$" × 4"

Y. $\frac{3}{16}$" clench bolts.

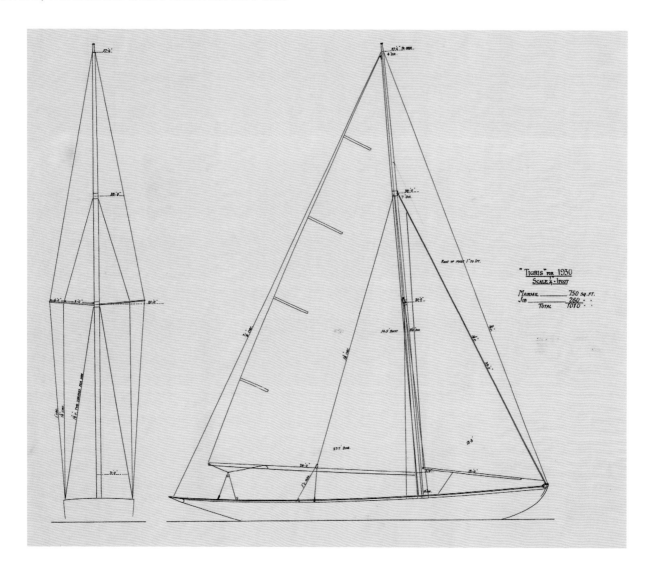

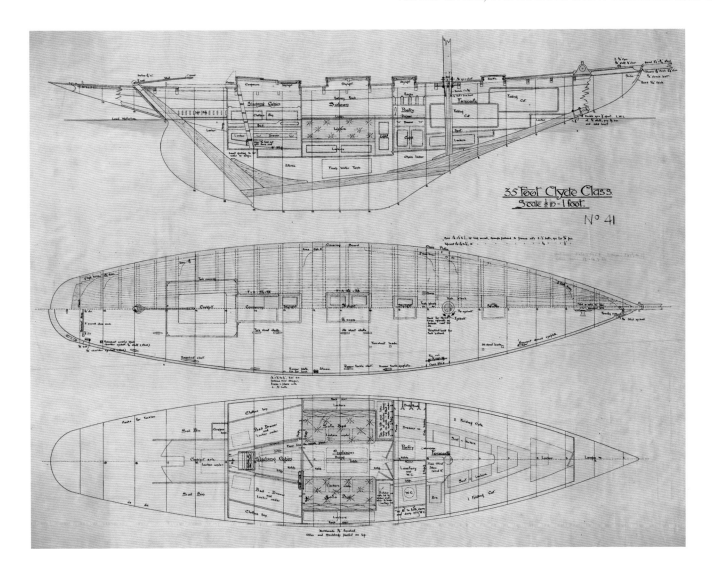

# CHAPTER 17

South Coast One Design

Design No. 85

(Sometimes called the Solent Class, though this is also the name of a much
smaller older class)

Length overall: 57 ft, 4 in.; 17.475 m.

Length waterline: 38 ft; 11.582 m.

Beam: 11 ft; 3.353 m.

Draft: 7 ft, 6 in.; 2.286 m.

Built in 1903.

In several respects, this is one of Mylne's most important early designs. In 1903 owners were getting disenchanted with yachts being built too light to survive several years of hard racing. They also disliked the low freeboard, which resulted in lots of spray and solid water on deck when the wind got up, not to mention limited headroom down below. It is relevant that oilskins and sea boots were nothing like as efficient as they are now, so owners and their friends got wet and cold more often and more severely than is the case these days. Right up to quite modern times, roughly about 1960, oilskins needed re-oiling regularly and after this process was complete, the garments were often sticky and awkward to get into or divest. No wonder there was a move to this sort of One Design class, where all

the yachts raced on equal terms and the design reflected the owners' wishes, not some handicapping rule that designers worked hard to circumvent in the search for speed.

The low freeboard of the raters and other racing craft was doubly serious because yachts had skylights to give light and ventilation down below. However, skylights were not sufficiently developed to be watertight till about the 1930s, and even then many were prone to let in too much water too often. Nowadays we can make skylights truly watertight by incorporating modern clamp-down hatches instead of the traditional wood frames that seldom had all-round rubber seals, together with effective clasps to pull the lids down extremely tight. To make matters worse, traditional skylights often had relatively weak glass. It is true there were brass bars over the glass in case anyone fell onto the skylight, but the bars were no protection against a dropped knife or shackle.

The South Coast One Design has sometimes been miscalled the Solent One Design, but that was a much smaller class from the drawing board of a different designer. To confuse things further, in the 1950s a new South Coast One Design was born. It is far smaller at 26 feet long, and again it became popular thanks to strict class rules and economical building, so that several builders turned out batches of these boats. This was yet another example proving that good One Design classes are a universal benefit and widely liked. Mylne's S.C.O.Ds were so well built that several are still hammering about the oceans, giving endless fun and excitement to owners and crew.

The lines plan is classically Mylne, and the hull shape has no straight lines apart from the underside of the counter and the side elevation of the transom. However, the counter is gorgeously shaped so that when the yacht starts to make speed, water runs up its full length before dropping away right aft in a curling stern wave. The transom is heavily curved athwartships and making it calls for some neat shipwrighting because the plank ends land on it at an awkward angle, and this angle varies from the centreline outwards. The transom could so easily have been designed flat, and this would have saved money, but it would have look far less lovely and been slightly weaker.

It is a feature of Mylne lines plans that the curves are 'all in the same family'. They seldom run parallel, yet they never wander far from their neighbours. This is the mark of a skilled designer and it helps to ensure that there are no ugly lumps of bumps or signs of unfairness anywhere. It may be argued that the bow and buttock lines, those fore and aft lines on the elevation drawing, closely match each other except amidships, where the lower one has a dip down amidships.

However, a more careful study shows that this dip is just a prolongation of the downward forward slopes and the upward aft ones. The dip is caused by the fullness of the hull, the extra width of the third waterline below the load waterline, halfway between the load waterline and the bottom of the keel. This is that famous Mylne characteristic, the 'full garboard'. It is appreciated by many yacht designers that it is an ideal way of disposing of the total volume of the yacht's hull. It gives space where it is so valuable for stowage and bilge water, and keeps the total width of the hull down, so as to improve windward sailing.

It is always fascinating to work out why some of these yachts have lasted so long. The construction plans tell a good part of the story. The stem is all in one piece and this eliminates a notorious danger area, where rot so often finds its way on board, at the join of the upper stem piece and the main length. Just as important, the overlap of the stem onto the keel is long and strong, with four heavy-duty bolts going through the ballast keel, the wood keel and the stem. In addition, there are nine thinner bolts gripping the stem onto the wood keel.

Just as important, every frame, including the bent timbers from the fore-end of the mast step, back almost to the aft end of the ballast keel, has a metal floor. As any sensible surveyor knows, if there is a shortage of floors in a yacht all sorts of troubles are likely to be found, especially leaking garboard planks, as these, the lowest of the planks, cannot withstand serious loads, and need ample help from the floors.

Although the hull has a lot of strength built into it, there are subtle signs of weight-saving. For instance most of the main frames are spaced 2 feet 3 inches, or 686 mm, apart. However, the gap between frame 3 and frame 4 is an extra inch, or 25 mm, greater, the next gap forward a further inch and the same again at the forward gap. This is because the frames are getting shorter as one moves forward, so they have lower overall stresses, and therefore they can be further apart. The same applies from the fore-end of the cockpit aft, where the stresses at sea will normally be less severe than further forward on the hull.

The chain plates are on the frame fronts so that the rigging screws can tilt in to line up with the inward slops of the shrouds. This also means that the bolts holding the chain plates lie fore and aft, and not through the planking. As a result, these bolts are less likely to get wet and so they tend to last longer. Of equal importance is the fact that bolt deterioration will not affect the planking in an area where it is highly stressed when sailing in bad weather.

The deck stringer that holds the beam ends is tapered both in depth and thickness at the ends. While a vertical reduction is often seen, even in cheaply built yachts, tapering the width as well is rare. It makes double sense since it reduces weight at the bow and stern, where a reduction is most effective, but it also makes fitting this big chunky lump of timber easier.

There is a secret in the midship section, an omission which tells a story. No bilge stringers are shown, nor do they appear on the

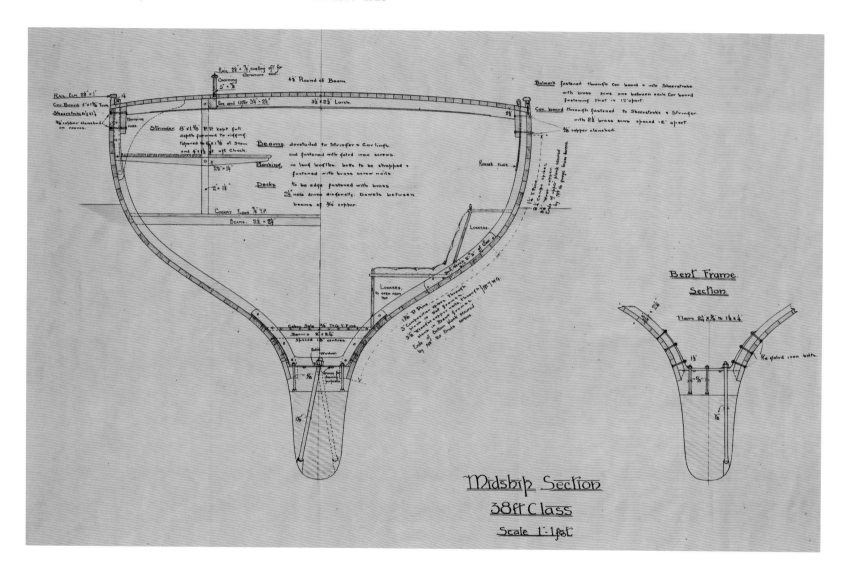

Midship Section

38ft Class

Scale 1"·1fot

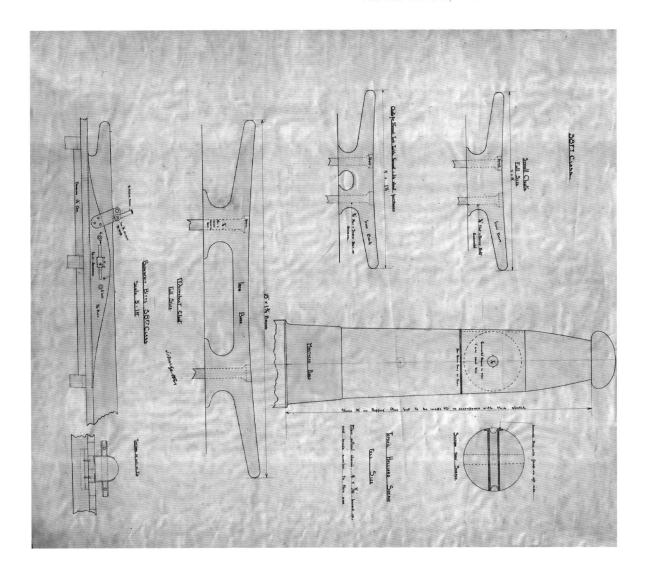

elevation construction plan, confirming that this omission is not a draughting error. Bilge stringers are the deep, thick fore-and-aft stringers that run almost the full length of the yacht very roughly in way of the waterline. They are often fastened at each frame and their total weight, including the fastenings, is significant. Some rival designers considered not having them as outrageous, and these yachts could not have been built under Lloyds' supervision because this august body disapproved of yachts built without these intermediate height stringers on each side.

Mylne seldom had any dealings with Lloyds, apart from when he built yachts to the International Yacht Racing Rules which dictated how 12-Metre, 8-Metre and 6-Metre yachts had to be built. The regulations for these International Classes stipulated that every yacht had to be built under Lloyds' supervision and to their detailed construction rules. These rules always included notes about the size of the compulsory bilge stringers.

One reason why he felt he was able to do so without supervision by Lloyds relates to Mylne's extensive experience and knowledge of yacht design and construction. Also, he considered that Lloyds was too inclined to adhere to traditional precepts without advancing with the times. There is also the widely held view that bilge stringers are most useful when a yacht runs aground and is left high and dry by a falling tide. Under these conditions the bilge may pound on the ground, so a strength component that helps to resist damage under these unusual circumstances may save the yacht from being destroyed. However, around the west coast of Scotland this sort of accident is much rarer than among the shallows of the east coast of England, for instance. So this is another facet of Mylne's tendency to omit these stringers.

In addition, he had some logic on his side. Bilge stringers are substantial fore-and-aft inboard planks located roughly halfway between the deck and the keel, and as such they are just about as badly placed as they could be to strengthen the vessel. An engineer considers a yacht to be a 'beam' with the deck forming the top flange and the keel forming the bottom one. These are where the structure needs the maximum amount of material. Roughly halfway between these two is the 'neutral axis', the place where material is not needed because it contributes little to the yachts overall strength. Planking is needed to keep out the water, and frames to hold the planks together, yet big fore-and-aft stringers make little sense here. Mylne had logic and technology on his side in his disagreement with Lloyds. In all this, it is important to remember that here we are discussing Lloyds Register and its rules. This is completely different to Lloyds the insurance underwriting organisation.

A most unusual thing on this class was the sliding doors at the cabin entrance. The idea has a lot of merit, because hinged doors can be dreadfully in the way in the cockpit and take up a lot of room. Doors can swing into the cabin, but this is widely considered bad practice because such an arrangement cannot stand up to a heavy breaking sea crashing aboard from aft. The doors are liable to burst inwards, followed by far too much salt water that causes distress and damage as it charges through the cabins.

In 1923, *Kelpie*, one of the class still sailing, was converted to a yawl with a smaller gaff mainsail, a titchy gaff mizzen and a thimble-headed topsail over the mainsail. The main mast was cut down to where the flying jib stay terminated. In 1933, another of the class, *Else IV*, changed to Bermudan rig with just a jib and staysail.

Some of the drawings of the fittings tell interesting stories. For instance, the main sheet cleats are shown as being of iron bark, 18 inches long and 1 ¾ inches wide, or 450 × 45 mm, with the middle hollowed out. This wood, which was specified for the other cleats, is as hard and wear resistant as its name suggests, rather rare and also tough to work. However, the middle cutaway makes the cleat look light and elegant. Just as important, it means that the sheet end can be knotted through the middle, so the rope cannot run right out by accident.

The saloon table was designed to stay level when the yacht heeled. There is a pivot at each end made of a bolt each with a nut and jam nut. By tightening the nuts, the friction between the swinging part of the table and the rigid upright supports is increased and the table swing is controlled. Without this, when the yacht is pitching about a lot, or rolling down wind, the table might swing with too much enthusiasm and throw the crockery, cutlery and glassware onto the cabin sole. It is typical of Mylne's technical knowledge and experience that the cabin table is secured down by two sets of three ⅜-inch brass bolts (10 mm) in brass sockets. This is an example of a simple reliable type of swinging table with the minimum number of parts.

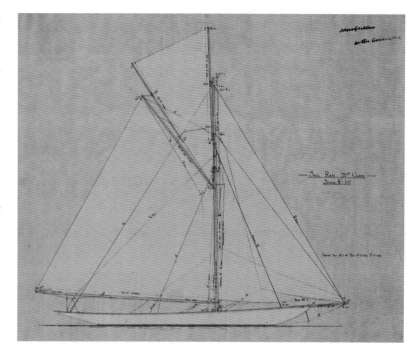

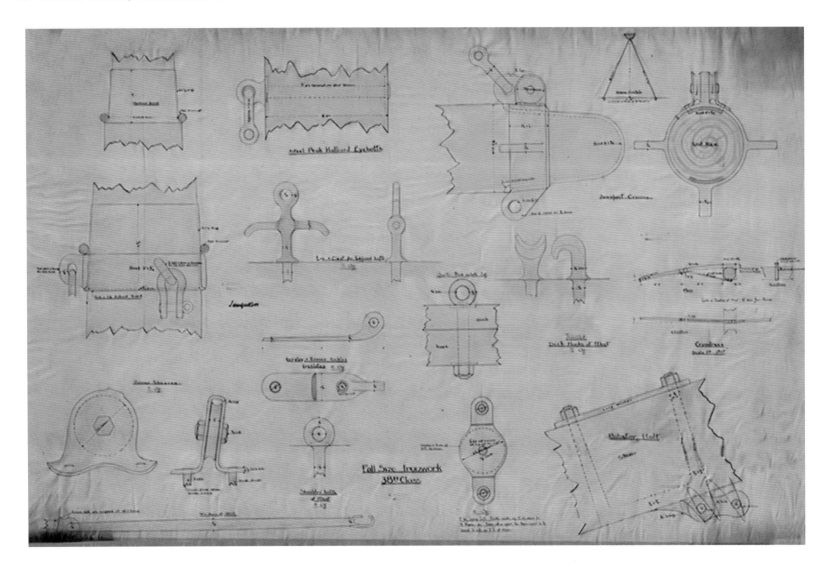

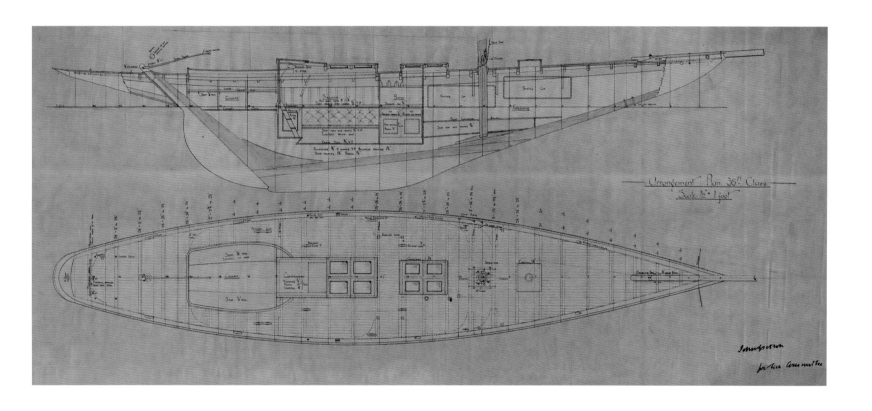

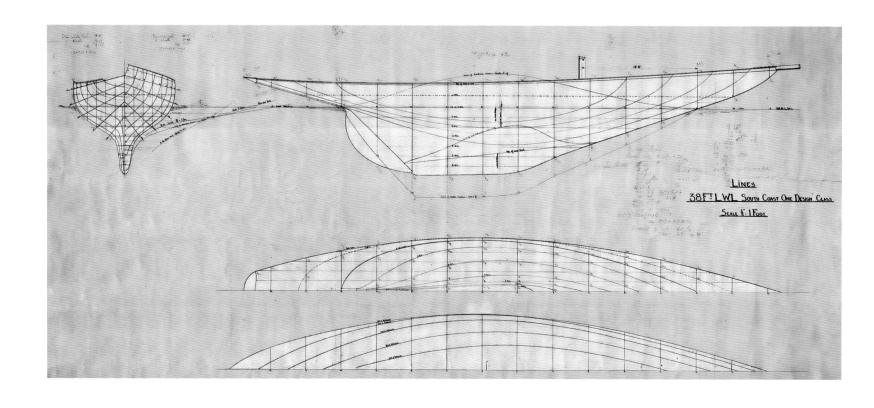

LINES
38 F.T L.W.L SOUTH COAST ONE DESIGN CLASS
SCALE ⅜ · 1 FOOT

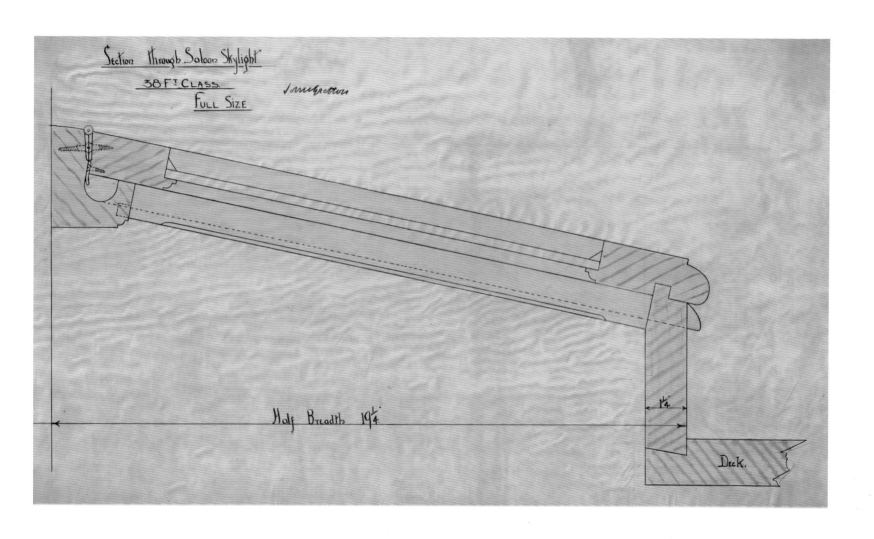

Section through Saloon Skylight
38 Ft Class.
Full Size

Construction

Half Breadth 19¼"

1¼"

Deck.

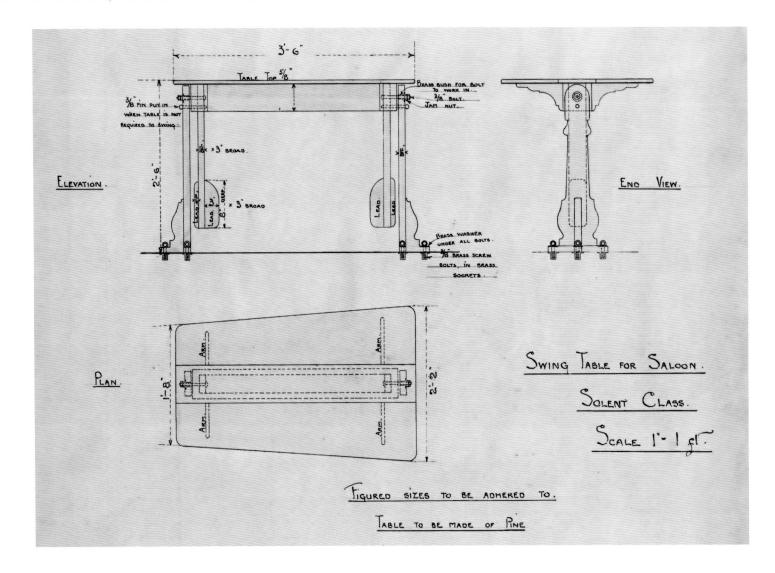

ELEVATION.

PLAN.

END VIEW.

SWING TABLE FOR SALOON.

SOLENT CLASS.

SCALE 1"- 1 FT.

FIGURED SIZES TO BE ADHERED TO.

TABLE TO BE MADE OF PINE

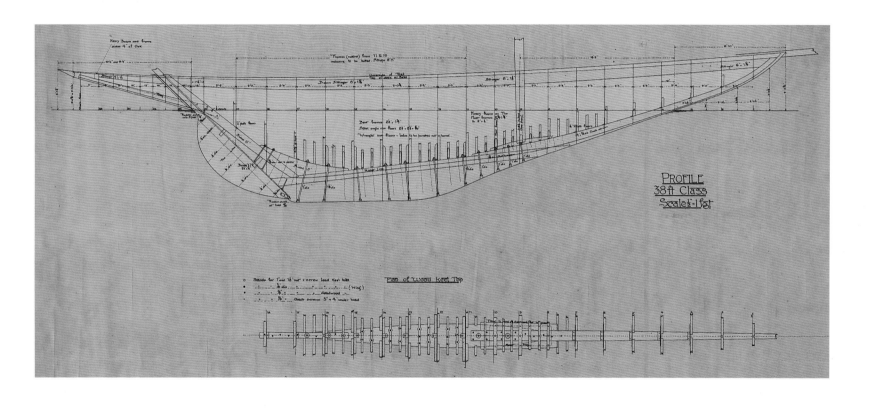

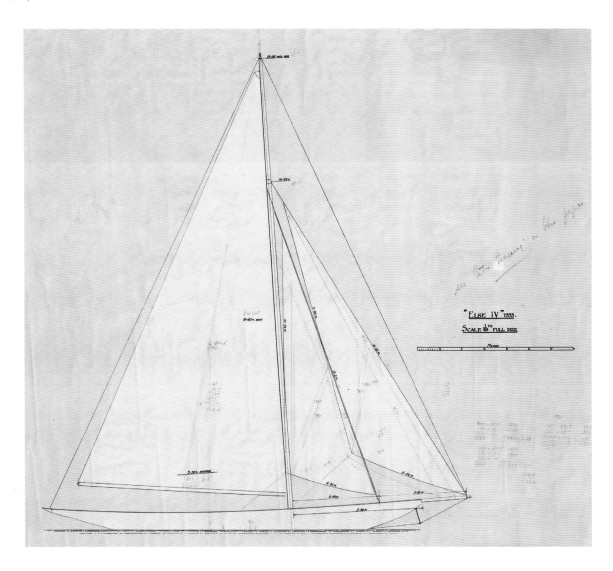

# CHAPTER 18

*Javotte* and *Kate* International 12-Metre Class
Design Nos 162 and 162A
Length overall: 60 ft; 18.29 m.
Length waterline: 39 ft, 9 ½ in.; 12.13 m.
Beam: 11ft, 1 in.; 3. 378 m.
Draft: 7 ft, 6 in.; 1.98 m.
Sail Area: ?
*Javotte* built by R. McAlister in 1909. At different times she was called *Baccarat*, *Betty II* and *Beduin II*. *Kate* was built by Philip Walwyn in 2006.

Early yachts built to the International Metre Rule had waterline lengths of about the same size as the class name. Hence a boat like *Javotte* was about 12 metres (39 feet) on the waterline, but soon designers saw that they could produce faster yachts by squeezing advantages from the Rule so as to end up with longer craft. Over the decades the overall length of International 12-Metre boats went from about 60 feet to around 72 feet. This increase in length occurs in every development class of sailing yacht where the overall length is not fixed at some firm limit because length means speed, except sometimes in very light airs.

The International 12-Metre class was popular right from the start because there was reasonable living space on board for the owner and three friends, plus the full paid crew. By having the backrests in the saloon made to hinge up along the top edge, this provided two more berths for the owner's party. With the six hands in the foc's'le, this gave a total of twelve people, enough to win races, though not so good in heavy weather. However, these yachts seldom raced far offshore and racing was usually postponed if conditions got wildly windy.

Right from the start of the class it was the practice to cruise from one regatta to the next, and by living on board, costs were kept down. Some owners would go back to work between regattas, leaving the paid crew to move the boat on to the next venue.

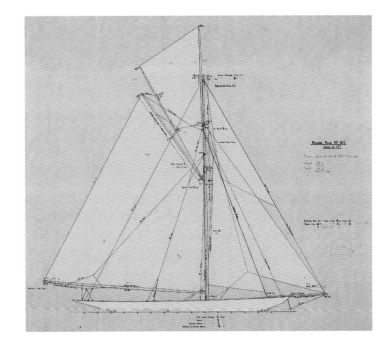

What made all the International Metre classes successful was the rule that decreed that construction must be to Lloyds specifications, and that body set out sensible scantlings that ensured each boat had a long life. As a result, when her racing days in the class were over an International Metre yacht had a new lease of life as a cruiser which often continued for decades.

Philip Walwyn approached Ian Nicolson, who was the senior partner at A. Mylne & Co. in 2001, with a view to buying a set of pre-1914 International 12-Metre drawings. Design No. 162 was chosen because *Javotte* was built to these plans and she was successful. Work soon started on the hull in Philip's spacious garden, on a small flat area surrounded by steep hillsides, on the tropical West Indian island of St Kitts. Philip is a most experienced and successful boat-builder, with more skill and experience than many professionals. He has built a succession of race-winning yachts for himself and gone off to steer them to many successes.

Philip named his yacht after his wife, Kate, who is an artist specialising in Caribbean scenes that are alive with the atmosphere of windswept, sun-drenched islands. Looking at one of her pictures evokes the sounds and smells of these unspoilt places. So while Kate was doing beautiful paintings, Philip was putting together another gorgeous work of art, built of laminated mahogany frames and cedar strip planks, all held together by epoxy glues. Bronze was used here, there and just about everywhere, including the chain-plates, sheet leads, and winches all in the true tradition. Bronze fabricated floors hold the frame feet to the keel and helped support the massive lead ballast keel. This was cast by Philip and his team of four young shipwrights using material salvaged from yachts sunk nearby during hurricanes.

Soon after she was launched, this yacht was on her mooring when she was hit by a 9,000-ton coaster built of steel. The yacht was unharmed, but a hole was punched in the metal plating of the freighter, so there is no doubt this is a very strong yacht.

The interior combines simplicity with practicality. Since no-one is going to do a lot of cooking, there is just a single burner cooker, well gimballed with a deep all-embracing fiddle to hold a pot or kettle in the worst weather. This must be the only yacht of this length with such a minimalist galley but Philip is an experienced seaman, having done many transatlantic voyages, so he knows where the emphasis should be – what is totally simple seldom goes wrong.

The rig is the same as *Javotte*'s original one, with gaff mainsail and a large jack-yard topsail. One small change was made for *Kate*, in that the gaff can be used as a boom for a Bermudan mainsail for short-handed long range cruising. In 1917 *Javotte* was given a Bermudan rig that was typical of the day, with the aft end of the boom away aft of the counter end and out of reach. This is not handy when reefing is required, and a modern rig would have a much shorter boom and no bowsprit, the way some old International 12-Metre yachts were redesigned when they became cruisers. After a few years with the original 12-Metre Class rig *Kate* was changed to a yawl. This meant that fearsome long heavy boom was shortened and short-handed sailing is now a great deal easier.

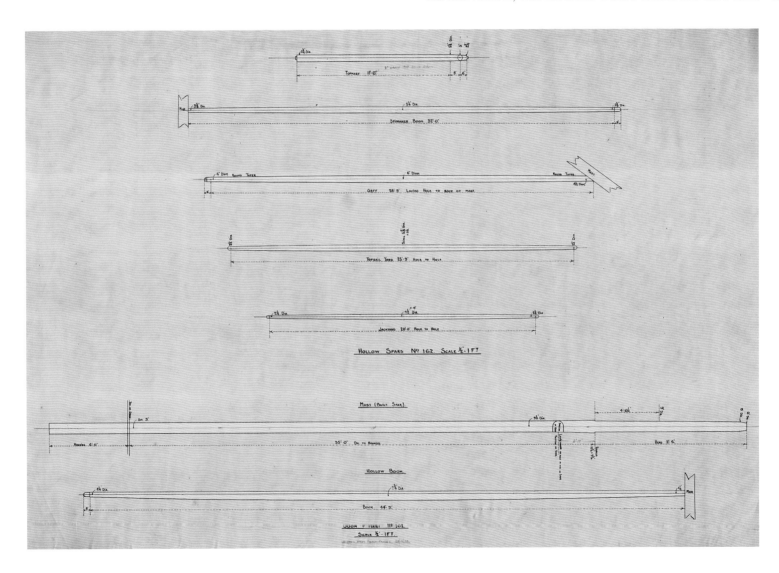

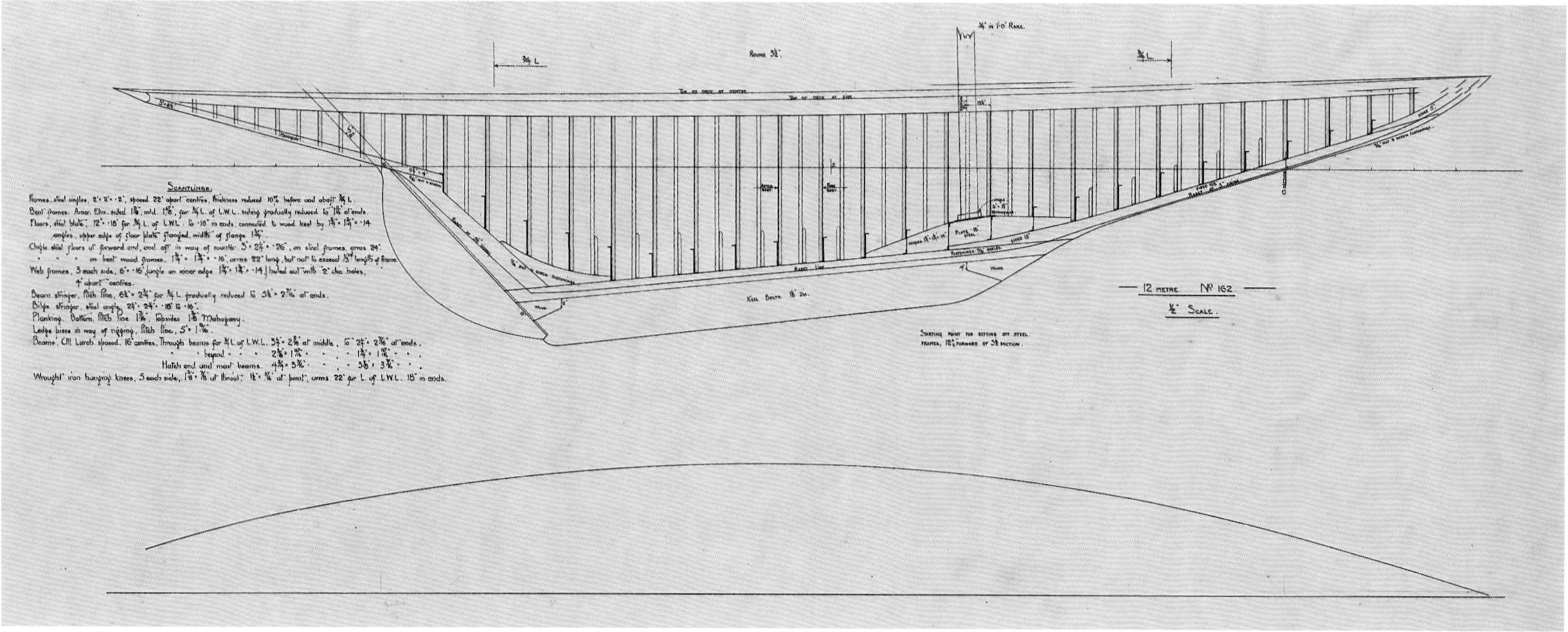
SCANTLINGS.
Frames, steel angles, 2" × 2" × ·2", spaced 22" apart centres, thickness reduced 10% before and abaft ¾ L.
Bent frames, Amer. Elm, sided 1⅜", mld. 1⅞", for ¾ L. of L.W.L. siding gradually reduced to 1⅛" at ends.
Floors, steel plate, 12" × ·18" for ¾ L. of L.W.L. to ·16" in ends, connected to wood keel by 1¾" × 1¾" × ·14 angles, upper edge of floor plate flanged, width of flange 1¾".
Web frames, 3 each side, 6" × ·16", 4" apart centres.
Beam stringer, Pitch Pine.
Bilge stringer, steel angle.
Planking, Bottom, Pitch Pine, Topsides Mahogany.
Ledge piece in way of rigging, Pitch Pine.
Beams, Oil Larch, spaced 16" centres.
Hatch end and mast beams.
Wrought iron hanging knees, 5 each side.
12 METRE No 162
½" SCALE.
KEEL BOLTS
RABET LINE
ROUND
STARTING POINT FOR SETTING OFF STEEL FRAMES

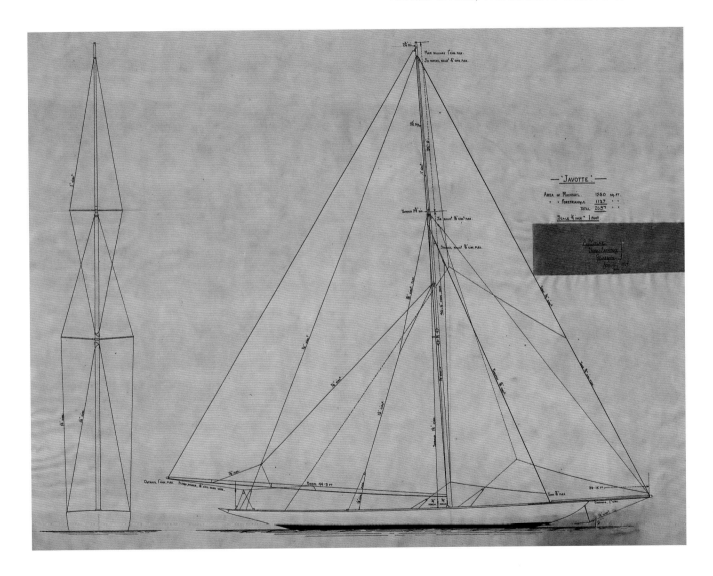

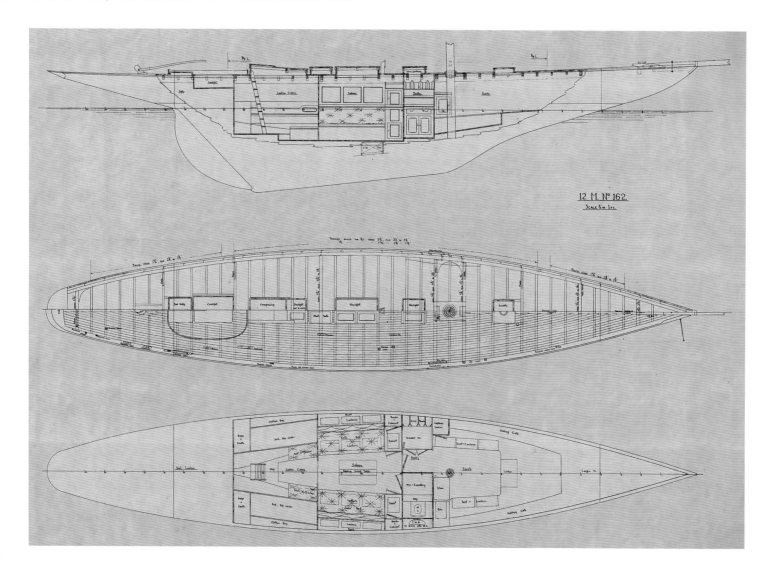

# CHAPTER 19

*Ostara* International 15-Metre-Class
Design No. 161
Length over deck: 75 ft, 2 in.; 22.911 m.
Length waterline: 49 ft, 7 in.; 15.133 m.
Beam: 12 ft; 3.658 m.
Draft: 9 ft, 3 in.; 2.819 m.
Built in 1909.

The only way to describe this yacht is stunning, sensational and superb. More than one wealthy man has thought about having a replica built but has backed off at the last moment, because it does need courage, as well as lots of cash, to own a yacht like this.

*Ostara* was built in 1909 to what is called the 'First International Rule'. These yacht racing regulations were launched in 1907 and produced some of the best racing afloat of all time. The 15-Metres were never numerically a big class, not just because they were expensive to build and maintain, but because there were not all that many men who could sail such craft. Skilled skippers, mates and plenty of experienced paid hands were needed to make these craft win races.

Each winter the whole fleet of '15s' were hauled up for a comprehensive refit. In the early spring they were launched and time was spent working up the crew and ensuring that the gear was going to stand up to the rough and tumble of racing. The captain and mate would decide when to reduce sail in a blow by the amount of bend in the spars, and if they got it wrong, something would break and solid lumps of wood, blocks and rigging would come hurtling down on deck. Just as serious, that was a lost race, and the crew got an extra week's wages or more when their yacht won. This mattered at a time when many of the paid hands had a tough time making a living during the winter by going fishing, sometimes in 16-feet-long (5 metre) open boats with no engines.

It is no coincidence that the length of the yacht apportioned to the owner and guests is about the same length as that allocated to the nine paid crew. Each side of the foc's'le was lined with four cot berths. These were made by bending 1 inch, or 25 mm, diameter galvanised steel tubes into a rectangle 6.5 feet long and 2 feet wide, that is 1.980 m × 610 mm. Onto this semi-rigid frame a canvas base was lashed to form a fairly comfortable sleeping shelf, which was folded up against the inside of the hull during the day when the crew used the seats each side.

The captain had the luxury of his own cot over the sail bin aft to starboard in the foc's'le and his own locker adjacent. In hot summer weather, like the rest of the paid hands, he had to suffer the discomfort of having the cooking stove giving out too much heat in the foc's'le when meals were being prepared, and sometimes long before and after cooking when hot water was needed. These large coal-fired stoves were standard fittings in yachts of this type, but not the most comfortable companions in such a confined space. Getting rid of the ash up the vertical ladder up through the fore hatch and overboard would call for skill and care just as loading aboard the coal, down the same awkward ladder, would need practice to avoid making a mess.

Everyone on these yachts tended to be far tougher than we are today. Oilskins and seaboots were nothing like as effective as modern ones and there is no protection for the crew or helmsman on deck. The low freeboard resulted in green deep water flooding aft along the deck when the yacht was plunging to windward in rough conditions, but at least for the owner and party that was half the fun. The sole concession to comfort was a pair of folding seats in the aft companionway at the aft end of the sleeping cabin, where two people could perch out of the wind and spray, looking out through the side windows or out through the hatch. However, sitting on the well-heeled windward seat would be exciting when the yacht was on her ear. With their vast sail areas these yachts lay far over when close hauled.

The cabin accommodation is a mixture of stark simplicity and touches of luxury. There is only one toilet for the owner's party. However, there is a writing table and two basins at the fore-end of the saloon, and this was important because communications were normally by letter, or by telegram which had to be written out, or by a hand-written note delivered by one of the crew. As a young man I can remember owners of big yachts sending written invitations to other yachts nearby on headed note-paper, with the owner's yacht club crest embossed and the yacht's name printed on the notepaper. My step-father started courting my widowed mother by such a hand-written note, delivered to our tiny cruiser by his paid hand. What could be more romantic, and so much more interesting than a crackling VHF radio message?

In the saloon and the aft sleeping cabin there are large bevelled mirrors. These look much smarter than ordinary plain-edged common mirrors, and are a sure sign of wealth being splurged in the best possible way.

The weight of such things was scarcely taken into consideration, but the two wardrobes at the aft end of the aft sleeping cabin had curtains in front instead of much heavier doors.

These yachts were in many respects pure racing machines. No engine was fitted, but they would go wonderfully well in the lightest breeze, helped by the vast topsails, set high, so high where there is often more wind than down at deck level.

For getting out of a small harbour, in a flat calm the yacht would sometimes be towed by four paid hands rowing the gig. This 20 × 4.5 × 1.9 foot light, slim rowing boat would be carried in davits in harbour, left ashore when racing and on the side deck when passage-making. At sea, in spite of its narrow beam it would have been a considerable nuisance, taking up most of the side deck and making getting forward difficult. The little dinghy would be over the main hatch when racing and over the skylight amidships when on passage.

These yachts were built to Lloyds Racing Yacht Rules, which explains why they were popular with owners because they were strong, watertight by the standards of their day and they did not depreciate fast. There were four extra-strong steel web frames with lightening holes closely spaced along the length of each frame. The principle frames and all the floors were steel, and the hanging knees were wrought iron. The latter material was put in a blacksmith's furnace till it was red hot then hammered to shape. Each of the long arms forming these strong knees were tapered towards the end in both thickness and width in the best engineering fashion.

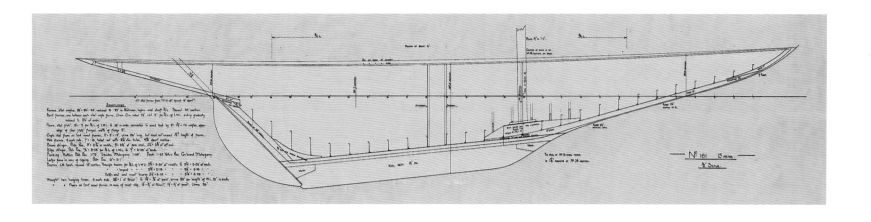

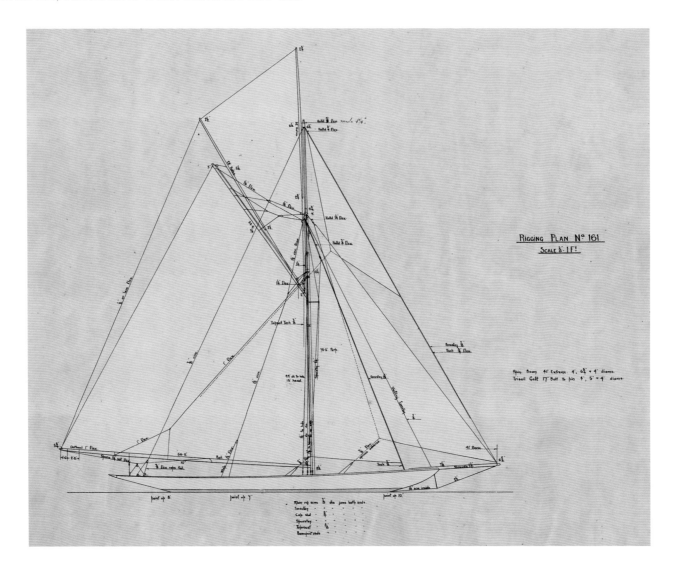

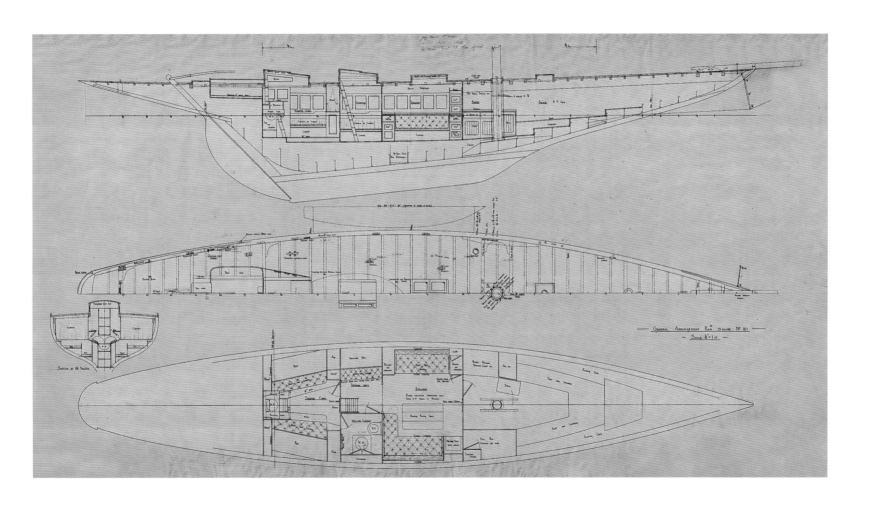

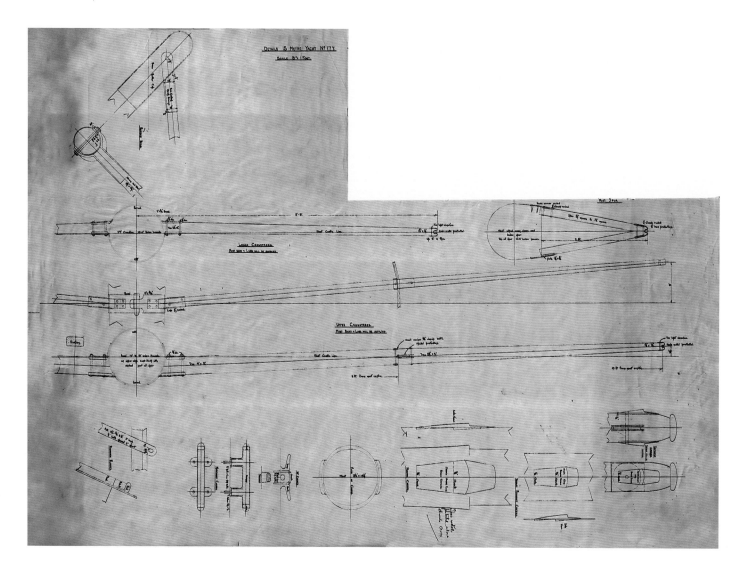

# CHAPTER 20

Motor Dinghy
Designs No. 171
Length overall: 14 ft, 6 in.; 4.42 m.
L.W.L.: 13 ft; 3.96 m.
Beam: 6 ft, 3 in.; 1.91 m.
Draft: 1 ft, 6 in.; 457 mm.

Before 1914, sailing yachts that had no engine would sometimes carry a launch like this for use as a mini-tug. This handy all-purpose power boat was used to get the yacht to the starting line for a race, or to pull her out of a cramped harbour when sailing out would be dangerous or impossible. The launch would also often be used for getting out to the yacht and back to the shore in the days when yachts were normally kept on a swinging mooring, often far from the beach and sometimes out in a swirling tide.

There are no flat areas on this elegant hull, and in this respect she is a typical Mylne design. Of course the transom is flat, but its perimeter is beautifully curved and its top edge has a lovely gentle camber. These boats were quickly and inexpensively built, so a transom curved when seen from above would never have been considered.

The sections on the left show that this would be an easy boat to build, as the turn of the bilge is nowhere too tight, so planking up would be easy. The frames were steamed and bent, and here again a soft curve at the waterline makes for easy shipwrighting. The bottom of the keel aft is well above the bottom of the propeller diameter, so a bronze skeg is fitted for protection and to support the aft end of the propeller shaft as well as the heel of the rudder. The underside of the rudder blade is just below the bottom of the skeg, so the designer has decided that responsive steering is more important than protecting the rudder blade if the boat goes aground aft. Normally, when getting ashore on a beach, only the bow would ground, and the crew would step off forward without the aft end of the boat getting chafed on the shore.

One reason for keeping the underside of the keel high aft is to ensure that the boat will turn in a tight arc. Also, the shallow keel saves weight, which is always such an important consideration when the launch has to be lifted aboard the parent yacht.

The sheer is delightfully curvaceous and relatively high aft, because the crew will normally sit aft of amidships and so the stern will be well down. This helps to keep the propeller immersed, an important consideration in rough weather. The engine in a boat like this before 1914 would typically be 4 hp or less. This is much better than two men rowing, one in each rowing position on the thwarts, because a man working continuously cannot generate much more than about one third of a horsepower, though for brief bursts he might generate 1 hp. However, a rower applies the propulsive force intermittently, and the boat feels no forward shove when the oar blade is being hauled forward for the beginning of the next stroke. So even a 2 hp engine would give a better speed than two men sweating and swearing hard.

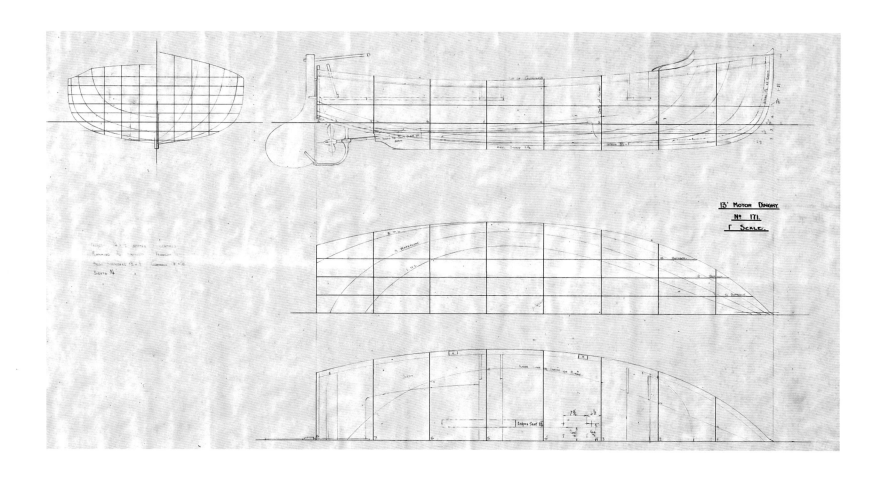

13' MOTOR DINGHY
Nº 171.
1" SCALE.

# CHAPTER 21

Kelvin Launch
Design No. 182
Length: 20 ft; 6. 096 m.
Beam: 4 ft, 4 in.; 1.321 m.
Maximum Draft: 1 ft, 7 in.; 483 mm.
Hull draft: 1 ft, 2 in.; 356 mm.
Displacement: 1882 lbs; 853 kgs.
Hull weight: 560 lbs; 254 kgs.
Engine: 448 lbs; 203 kgs.
Fuel (full load in tank): 56 lbs; 25 kgs.

A hundred years ago, the Scottish engine firm that makes the famously reliable Kelvin engines wanted to increase sales and came up with the idea of commissioning a variety of designs for launches. The firm then organised the building of these different sizes and types at boatyards all over the country. Each boat had a Kelvin engine in it so sales burgeoned. Before the First World War, and even after the Second World War, these launches were to be found all over the worldwide British Empire.

Some were working far up rivers, where their shallow draft was such an asset. Some were used by governors and managing directors to go to work or inspect districts, plantations or farms. In the tropics these boats had elegant canvas awnings with scalloped edges and local people in appropriate uniforms as crew. Some were ship's boats, used on superb steam yachts or merchants ships. This design is special because the beam is so narrow. There are two reasons for the modest beam-to-length ratio. The first idea is to make this a very easily driven craft so that a small engine will give a reasonable speed with economy. The second, just as important, is that ship's and yacht's launches had to fit in the narrow spaces over the side decks between the deckhouses and the ship's side.

The lines of this sleek launch show an easily propelled craft, fine forward and with plenty of reserve buoyancy aft to prevent squatting when the throttle was fully opened and the boat was well loaded. There is some flair forward to discourage spray from coming aboard, but nowhere are the lines sharply curved, not even at the tightest turn of the bilge. Also, there is virtually no tumblehome so this will be an easy boat to build, using wood planking and frames or any other boatbuilding material for that matter.

For engine efficiency the propeller must not be tiny, so it has to project below the line of the keel. It is protected by a metal skeg that doubles as the bottom support of the rudder. It is interesting to see that the tip clearance of the propeller is less than the normally recommended 12 per cent of the propeller diameter. Some designers aim for a 25 per cent clearance between the propeller blades and the underside of the hull, but with shallow draft launches this is seldom achievable, and, as so often in the world of naval architecture, the designer has to accept a compromise.

The boats built to this design were pretty, with their highly curvaceous forward breakwater and boldly shaped forward seats. Though the general arrangement plan shows there are pairs of knees on top of the amidships thwart, a pencil note on the general arrangement plan confirms that in practice these knees were fitted under the thwart. This complicated the construction, but gives more sitting space on this important thwart. At the bow and stern there are lifting rods so that davits falls can quickly and easily be hooked on to lift the launch out of the water, or put her afloat. As the rods are gripped at deck level there is no chance of the boat turning over as she is lifted, even though the load is taken down at the keel below the centre-of-gravity. This low location is where the boat's strength is excellent.

The two-cylinder Kelvin petrol engine was hand started and had an entirely separate gear-box, as was common before 1914. Looking at the plans it seems that the helmsman might have stood right aft and steered with a tiller. However, the gear lever and throttle were forward of the amidships thwart, so it is likely that there was a steering wheel fixed on the inside of the gunwale, with its axle athwartships. This is not shown on this plan, but modifications after construction have always been common on launches and yachts. Kelvins made steering gear as well as engines and these launched were intended to boost the firm's total sales, so many had Kelvin steering wheels and linkages.

The fuel tank was originally to be 24 × 6 × 10.5 inches (610 × 152 × 267 mm), however the designer decided to go for a wider shallower tank, 30 × 5 × 10.5 inches, which is 762 × 127 × 267 mm. The fore-and-aft dimension has to be unchanged to suit the width of the thwart. In the event that the engine failed or ran out of fuel, there are a pair of rowlock sockets aft of the amidships thwart and a pair of stout ash oars would be stowed in many of these launched.

Launches for ships and yachts were used each day to collect food from the shore, since refrigerators were not widely used and not capacious. This meant that daily shopping was common, and sometimes cooks would shop in the morning for lunch and again in the afternoon for dinner. To get the food out to the boat without having it soaked with spray there are lots of lockers at the bow and stern. To deal with flying spray, many of these launches had folding canvas hoods forward and aft.

The cushions were 2 inches, or 50 mm, thick, whereas now most boats have 3-inch or 750-mm-thick cushions. Some people will say this confirms we are 50 per cent flabbier than our ancestors!

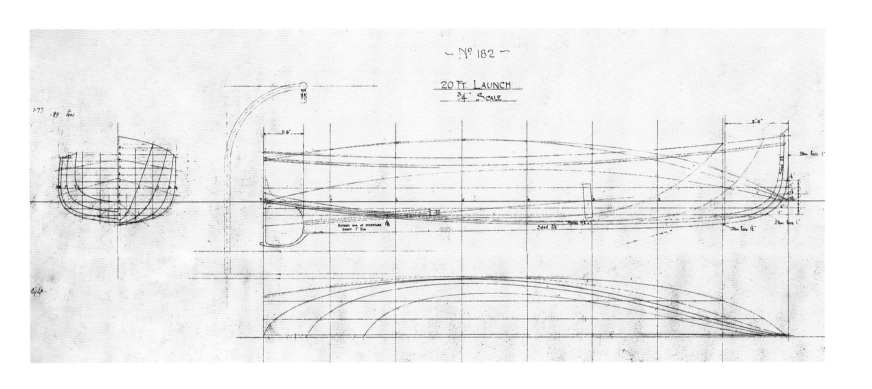

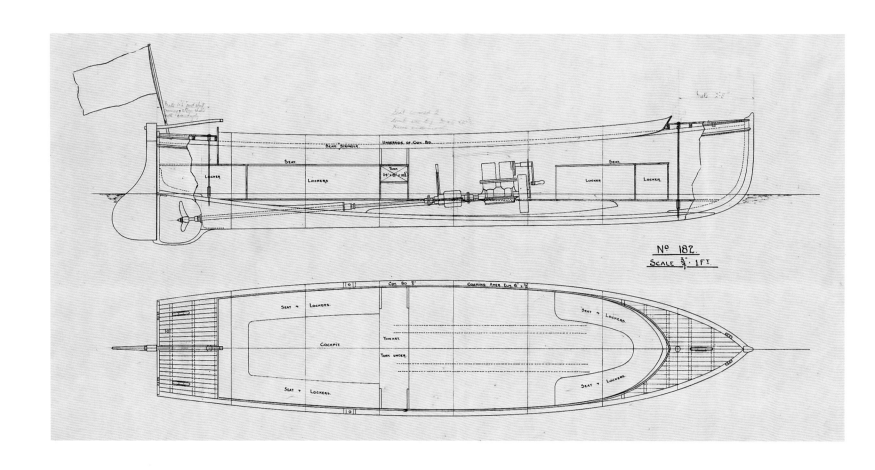

Nº 182.
Scale ¾" : 1 FT.

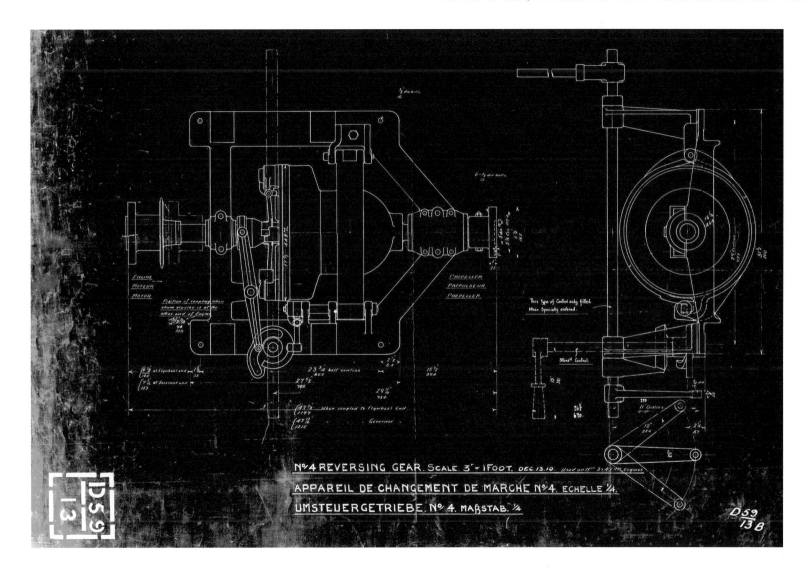

Nº 4 REVERSING GEAR. SCALE. 3" = 1 FOOT. DEC. 13.10. *Used on Nºs 3 & 4 HP Engines.*

APPAREIL DE CHANGEMENT DE MARCHE Nº 4. ECHELLE ¼.

UMSTEUERGETRIEBE. Nº 4. MAßSTAB. ¼.

# CHAPTER 22

*Amazon*

Design No. 174

Length overall: 39 ft, 6 in.; 12.04 m.

Length waterline: 37 ft, 6 in.; 11.43 m.

Beam: 9 ft; 2.73 m.

Draft: 3 ft, 2 in.; 965 mm.

Built by Smiths of Tighnabraich in 1910.

Considering *Amazon* was built in 1910, she was ahead of her time in that she had a snug wheelhouse where the helmsman could be comfortable regardless of the notoriously cold wet Scottish weather. Like all the early wheelhouses there is not much space inside, and it is probable that the paid hands did most of the steering and navigating or, rather, pilotage work, for this sort of vessel would mainly be operating in close coastal waters.

The foc's'le shows only one folding cot berth, but it is likely there were two people living up forward. The owner and his party would enjoy the snugness of the saloon aft, well clear of the engine noise. The three full-width bulkheads ensure the gentle chuff-chuff of the 2-cylinder Gardner paraffin engine would scarcely be heard aft. This engine going flat out only did 600 revolutions per minute, and it was hand started. The large flywheel, 6 inches, or 150 mm, thick in a fore and aft direction and over 2 feet, or 600 mm, in diameter would need some impetus to get it

going, but once it was whirling round, its momentum ensured smooth running and by modern standard the engine noise would be subdued. By 1923, the engine had been replaced by a four cylinder one by the same maker. The designer wisely drew an engine room with plenty of space, so that fitting the larger power unit presented few problems.

Not shown on the plans is any outside or inside ballast. However, the rigging plan shows four sails and there is a lot of top hamper, so it is certain some extra weight was carried low down in the form of pigs of iron or lead internal ballast. An interesting detail is the rake of the masts and funnel, with the foremast having a ⅞ inch rake per foot length, which is just over 1 in 14. However, the funnel rakes 1 in 12, and the aft mast less than 1 in 11. The aim here is to follow the well-known dictum that if one wants to ensure the masts do not appear to taper together, then their rake must increase as one goes aft. In contrast, commercial vessels were traditionally designed in a rush to save money and the draftsmen used to use the back of their tapered set-squares to draw in the amount of aft tilt. As a result, all the rakes tended to be the same for the funnels and masts and from abeam they would tend to look as if they had converging rake angles.

An unusual feature of this power yacht is the stepping of the mizen mast, on deck. Considering that there was a mizzen sail and mizzen staysail, the down-thrust of the mizzen mast would not be negligible. This is in contrast to the main mast which lodged down on a wooden mast step on top of the keel, in what was then the conventional way.

The skylight aft of the funnel is cleverly fitted so as to give simultaneous light and ventilation to the aft saloon, the lavatory and the pantry, which forms half of the galley. In the days when this yacht was built, skylights were very common. By the end of the Second World War in 1945 they were more or less totally discarded, partly because it was so hard to stop them leaking even in moderate weather. In addition, even

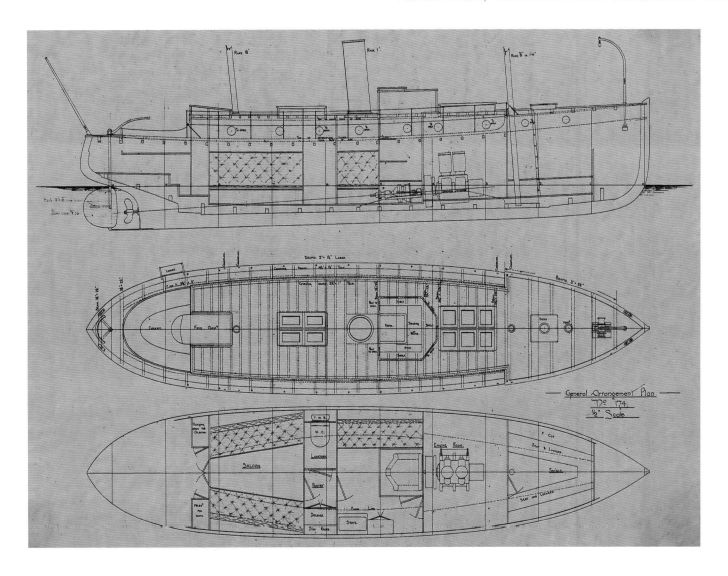

General Arrangement Plan.
No. 174.
½" Scale.

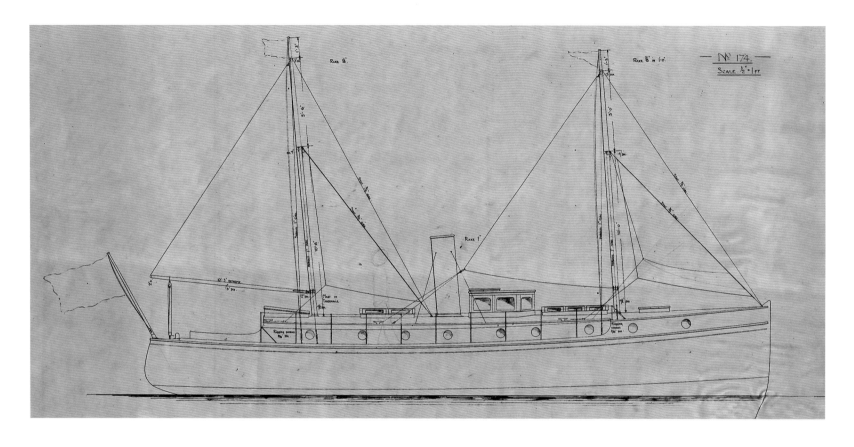

when there were guard bars across the glass these panels got broken too often and then the water, in the form of spray and rain, poured in.

With her small draft, spacious engine room, wide long deck spaces and good steadying rig, it is easy to see why someone would want to build a yacht like this today. She would go far on a small amount of fuel, she would be restful and comfortable and she would be able to enter tiny harbours and shallow creeks. She could be a fun power yacht to own and be economical to run. She could be built of wood, like the *Amazon*, or steel or aluminium or fibreglass, and give unlimited pleasure to any owner and all his family.

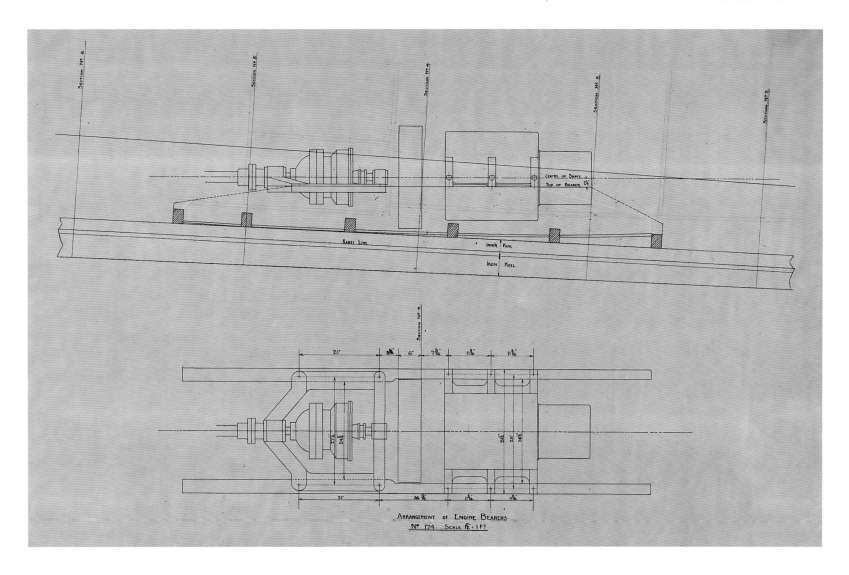

ARRANGEMENT OF ENGINE BEARERS
No 174    SCALE 1½" = 1 FT

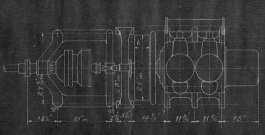

2 E.H.M. GARDNER ENGINE & REVERSING GEAR WITH PROPELLER SHAFT & STERN TUBE

| ENGINE GARDNER | 2 E.H.M. |
|---|---|
| POWER | |
| R.P.M. | 600 |
| SIZE OF EXHAUST | 2¼in |
| " WATER | 1in |
| " FEEDWATER | 2⅛in |
| DIA. OF CYLINDERS | 4½in |
| STROKE | 7in |
| TOTAL HEIGHT | 33⅝in |
| " LENGTH | 97⅝in |
| " WIDTH | 38⅝in |
| DIA. OF SHAFT | 2in |

NORRIS & HENTY
ENGINEERS
87 Queen Victoria Street EC

Scale = 1" = 1 foot

DRAWING Nº 115 A

# CHAPTER 23

*Etive*

Design No. 217

Length overall: 45 ft; 13.72 m

Length waterline: 43 ft, 1 in.; 13.13 m

Beam: 9 ft, 6 in.; 2.90 m.

Draft: 3 ft, 10 in.; 1.17 m.

Built by Robertson's of Sandbank, Argyll in 1912.

What makes this day launch interesting is the ruthless simplicity and efficiency of the design. There are no complications to baffle the builder. The forward 18 feet 6 inches (5.64 metres) of the load waterline is a straight line, and its angle off the centre-line is a mere 11 degrees. This ensures the hull slides effortlessly through the water, even though the engine is only a modest two-cylinder paraffin one. At the maximum beam the waterline width is far less than the deck width to keep down the hull shape resistance. There is a long straight length of keel, which will ensure that this yacht keeps tracking in a straight line without constant attention to the helm. However, the keel terminates 6 feet, or 2 metres, forward of the propeller, so there is an excellent flow of water aft. The propeller diameter is 2 feet 9 inches, or 840 mm, so it scoops up lots of water for every turn, and shows that the designer appreciated that

large slow-turning propellers are best when the available horsepower is small, as it almost always was before 1914.

This boat was built in what might be described as a typical pre-First World War style without many concessions to safety. For instance, the ladder from the cockpit to the main foredeck has no grab rails and the stanchions with their single guardrail stop short of the aft end of the top deck. To get to the saloon, one walks through the engine room that has no barrier between the busy machinery and the passing crew. There is a skylight in the engine room, but the indications are that it is semi-portable. Its secondary use was to make it easy to lift the engine out of the boat.

Right forward there is a large anchor davit for lifting the anchor on deck, once it has been hauled up to the sea surface. When this yacht was built it was common practice to have big heavy anchors because engines were not fully reliable, and when they failed the anchor was the last hope if the wind was on shore. There were no radios so the crew could not yell for help every time they had a little trouble. To accompany the pair of large anchors there would have been lots of galvanised chain, as the large size of the anchor locker confirms.

The first owner of this yacht was Ian T. Nelson and he got the Mylne office to design not only the boat, but also its boathouse and launching facilities at Loch Etive. The mobile cradle on the marine railway was made of pitch pine, that finest of soft woods. It was stiffened with steel cross-beams, brackets and diagonals. What is remarkable is that the athwartships bearers of the cradle, which support the boat, are only 10 feet 9 inches, or 3.28 metres, between the extreme fore and aft points. This shows the boat must have been strong to survive without the hull bending on such a short length of supporting structure.

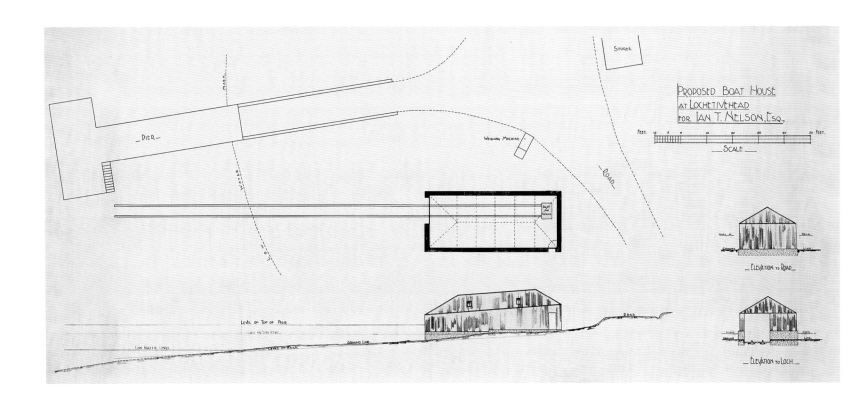

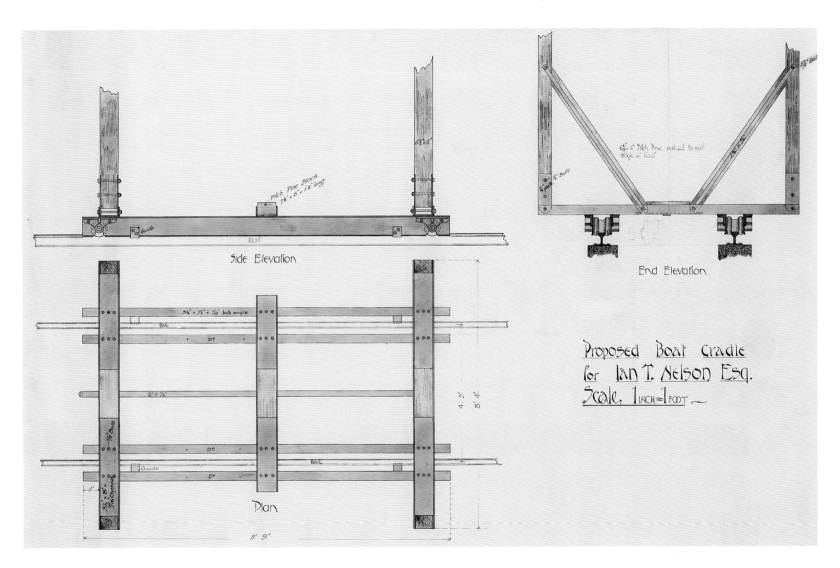

Side Elevation

Plan

End Elevation.

Proposed Boat Cradle
for Ian T. Nelson Esq.
Scale, 1 INCH = 1 FOOT.

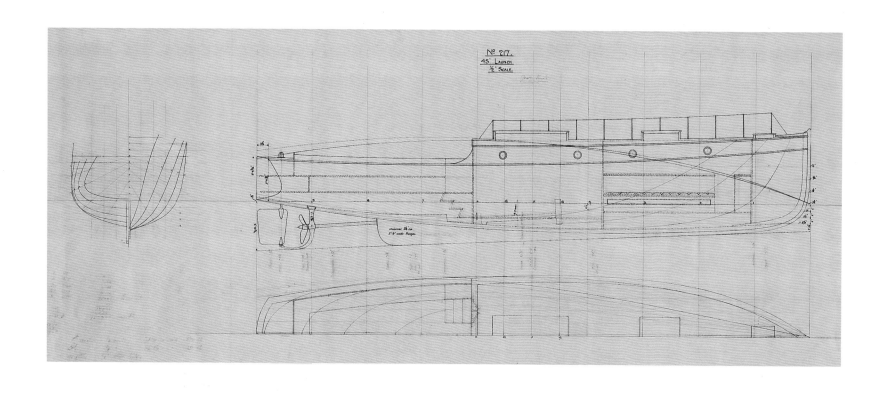

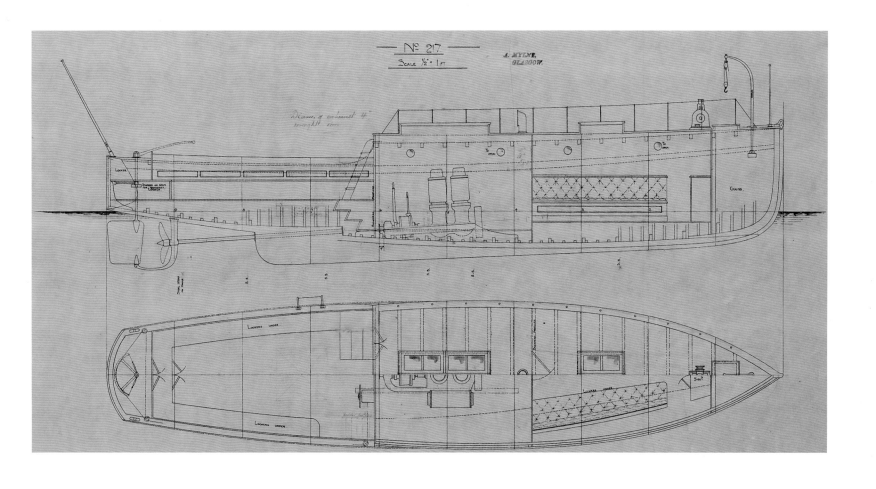

# CHAPTER 24

*Narwhal*
Design No. 61
Length overall: 50 ft; 15.24 m.
Length waterline: 46 ft, 3 in.; 14.10 m.
Beam: 9 ft, 6 in.; 2.90 m.
Draft: 4 ft, 6 in.; 1.37 m.
Built 1901 by R. McAlister and Son, Dumbarton. Official Number 113112.

*Narwhal* encapsulates the essence of the pre-1914 steam yacht in miniature. She has the fine lines and narrow width of an easily driven hull pushed along by a large slow-turning propeller that is so big that when stationary, its tip is on the waterline. With a fast-turning propeller connected to a light high-revving engine, one cannot have the propeller so high as it will race wildly when the stern is high out of the water. This over-revving can cause enormous damage to hull and engine and can be hard to control.

The engine room, with its lumpy boiler, two large side bunkers and two big tanks, takes up almost one third of the length of the useable space in the yacht. Aft of the cockpit, the counter is so shallow there is little room for anything except the reversed quadrant on top of the rudder stock and some stowage for warps and fenders. The cockpit is where the owner and his small party would spend plenty of time while one of the paid hands steered, and another prepared the next meal and served drinks.

The low narrow foc's'le would be tolerable for the crew of two, and maybe a boy as well, because in effect they often worked just from Friday evening till Sunday evening. Sometimes their working 'week' did not start till lunchtime Saturday, if the owner worked on Saturday morning, as so many people did pre-1914, and indeed for many years thereafter.

It is instructive that there is no door in the watertight bulkhead between the foc's'le and the cabin, even though the pantry was at the aft end of the cabin. So to lay the table for a meal the steward would have to toil up the steep foc's'le ladder, and down the slightly less steep saloon steps. The food would travel the same route because the cooking stove was in the foc's'le. The deck plan does not show a food locker, with jalousies all round, to act as a larder but there would almost certainly be one, or maybe two, one for meat and one for vegetables.

The engine room is half filled by the boiler, and this component was in several respects the downfall of the steam yacht. Boilers were prone to leaks especially when aged, which meant a loss of pressure and hence speed and endurance. They needed almost constant feeding with coal, and the fire had to be riddled as well as resupplied, sometimes in rough sea conditions, so this was not a job for the unskilled. The ash had to be taken from the bottom of the fire box and up the ladder on deck, then heaved overboard, without soiling or singeing the immaculate wood decks. Paid hands needed to be tough.

About 1925 the steam engine was taken out and a Pickford-Tyler four-cylinder paraffin engine fitted. This would have increased the noise level on board, but freed off a great deal of space for living accommodation. It also meant that the paid crew were less busy by a large margin, as there was no more stoking and probably no more standing by the engine controls for the whole time the yacht was under way. However, the yacht would no longer have plenty of spare steam to blast through the siren, giving a strident sound heard a mile or more away. This ability to make a lot of noise was a safety feature of these steam yachts and handy for giving warning, for instance when entering a crowded harbour in the dark or during a rainstorm.

The helmsman would normally be one of the paid crew and he stood behind the funnel, so his view forward was less than ideal. If there was an awkward gust of wind, the smoke and soot from the funnel could easily blacken his uniform and cause him to cough and splutter. When manoeuvring he probably called down to the engine room for more or less speed, or for reverse. At least the almost silent steam engine would not prevent the man working as engineer (as a relief from being cook or stoker or deck-hand) from hearing the commands.

The single mast was not just for decoration. It carried a modest size of headsail which would be enough to flatten out a lot of rolling and so make life aboard more comfortable. It was also important for flying the correct flags, and when this yacht was built, flag etiquette was carefully practiced and universally considered important. Flags were hoisted in the morning, taking a lead from the senior or largest yacht on the moorings, and lowered all together in the evening, following the same procedure. Paid hands went on deck in good time and stood around, sometimes in the driving rain and cold, till the precise correct time.

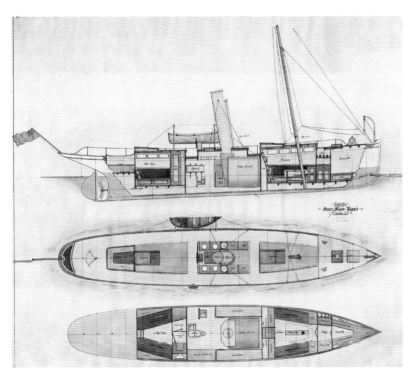

*Narana*
Design No. 47
Length overall: 51 ft; 15.55 m.
Length waterline: 45 ft; 13.72 m.
Beam: 10 ft; 3.05 m.
Draft: 4 ft, 5 in.; 1.35 m.

At first sight, *Narana* looks like *Narwhal* on the previous pages. She has the same sensible construction with full-width beams over each end of the engine room. Many a designer has unwittingly produced a weak vessel by having long cabin tops, which take away so much of the vessel's strength. When there are too few strong beams extending from deck-edge to deck-edge, without the interruption of a cabin top, the hull is like a box with no lid firmly attached. The lack of a long, strong deck results in the whole vessel distorting then leaking, but this shouldn't happen to *Narana*.

There is the same long slender counter which is elegance personified. It also provides reserve buoyancy aft and reduces the chances of having a wave tumble into the aft cockpit. The counter, round-ended in plain view, would have been the devil to build, as the planks would need twisting and bending at the same time. However, the shipwright's skills when this yacht was launched were phenomenal, and Clyde builders were world famous.

The bigger diameter of the funnel indicates a larger boiler, and hence more power and speed than *Narwhal*. In severe weather out at sea sometimes ships lost their funnels, due for instance to the wires shrouds being rusty and overdue for replacement. The consequences could be dire, what with the loss of uptake draft and the chances of waves getting through the gaping hole in the deck, quite apart from the damage caused by a large steel tube charging about on deck.

This funnel is raked aft by 2 ¼ inches per foot length, whereas the mast is only raked 2 inches. This difference is to make the mast and funnel appear to slope back the same amount. Only an experienced yacht designer knows about this subtle trick. The steep rake of the mast meant that no permanent backstay or runners were needed as the shrouds prevent the mast toppling forward.

The single small sail was not meant primarily as a safety measure because steam engines were so reliable. Its main purpose was to damp down rolling, since a narrow yacht of this type, with a well-rounded bilge, would have a tendency to swing from side to side with little provocation. However, a sail of the size shown is a wonderful roll-killer. It does not eliminate the vice, but it tends to slow the roll and also reduce the arc. Sometimes a sail will almost wipe out that part of the swing on the windward side, so instead of rolling, say, 25 degrees each side of amidships, the roll might be down to 10 degrees to windward and 20 degrees to leeward. This reduction from a total of 50 degrees to 30 degrees may not seem much, but for anyone trying to enjoy a quiet drink and a game of cards, or for one of the crew struggling in the galley, the difference would seem large and a great pleasure.

The helmsman stood on deck aft of the engine room deck-house, his view forward badly blocked by the large funnel and also the two fat cowl vents abeam of the funnel. In practice a vessel like this, with a long straight keel, will hold her course for minutes if the helmsman lets go of the steering wheel and ambles athwartships to one or other of the side decks, to get a better view forward and see what the yacht was about to hit.

The motive power is a three-cylinder engine, each cylinder having a diameter to match the pressure in it, shown by the small, medium and large diameter circles.

On the port side of the main engine is a little steam engine driving a water pump. On the opposite side a work bench is fixed over a water tank, and a good crew would be forever beavering away on maintenance jobs using this long bench. The intelligent ones would know that if they could minimise the work which had to be done by a shipyard every winter there was a better chance the owner could go on affording to run the yacht and employ them. Though wages were low, and many materials were cheap, running a yacht of this size called for a substantial income. The whole of the outside, above and below the waterline, had to be fully repainted every spring. The varnished parts needed rubbing down between each application, and good crews applied four coats each spring. They also did lots of revarnishing on fine summer days, during the summer, to keep up the appearance of the yacht and reduce the work needed each winter.

Slung from the port davits is a double-ended dinghy. The men who made these little boats specialised in them and knew all manner of tricks to coax the planks to bend so sharply round to the stern-post. Included in their repertoire were such ploys as subtly thinning the planks at the point of greatest curvature, and using heat with the greatest care.

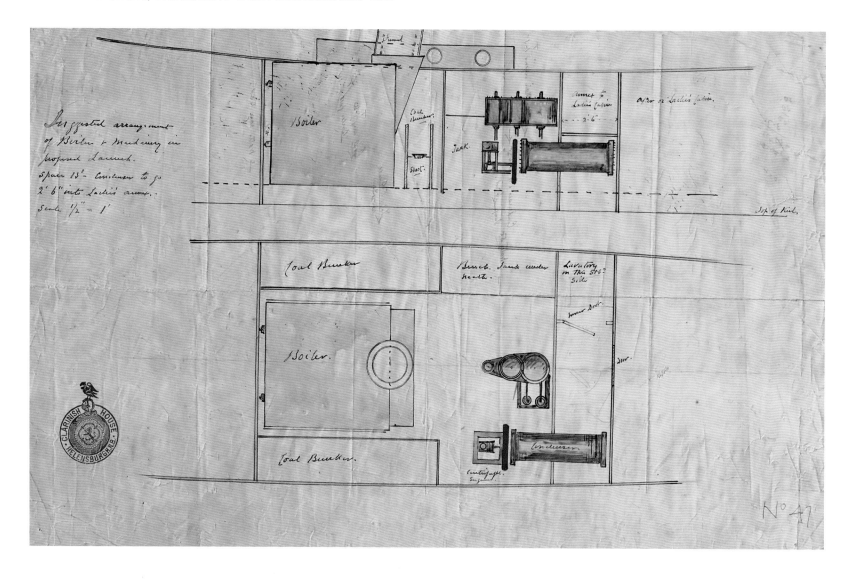

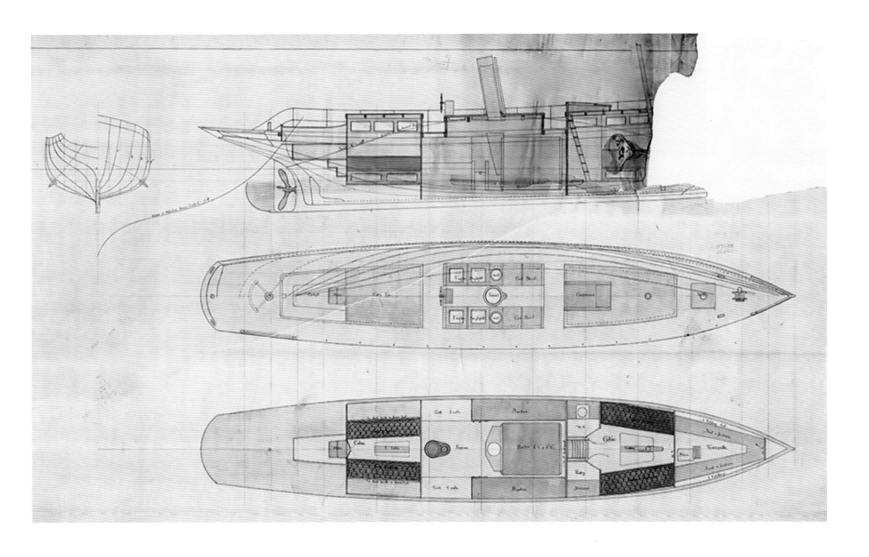

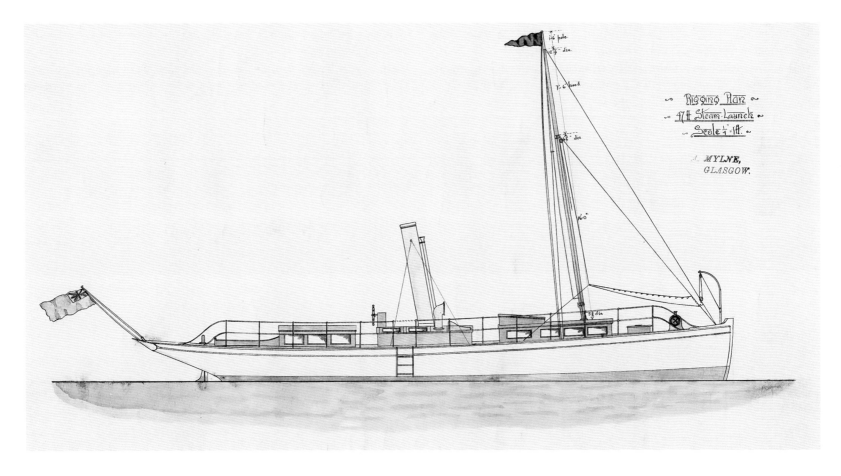

They would also pre-bend the planks by fixing one end down on a bench and tying heavy weights on the overhanging end, so that the wood slowly took up a permanent curve before any work was done on it.

It's easy to see that this dinghy is of the best quality, not just because she has that expensive pointed stern, but also because she has double instead of single knees on the thwarts, also a shaped grating in the bow and another aft. The parent yacht also has a curvaceous grating across the stern, showing this was not a cheaply built yacht.

The accommodation is more comfortable than in the slightly smaller *Narwhal*. There is a proper galley, separated from the crew's foc's'le by a curtain. Double doors lead into the saloon so the food could be put on a tray and taken quickly from the stove to the table. The aft cabin has a cloakroom forward on the port side. This is in effect a walk-in wardrobe opposite the toilet space. This accommodation drawing is so detailed, the draughtsman has even drawn in the locks on the toilet doors.

# CHAPTER 25

*Galma*

Design No. 150

Length overall: 60 ft, 4 in.; 18.390 m.

Length waterline: 59 ft, 1 in.; 18.009 m.

Beam: 13 ft; 3.962 m.

Draft: 4 ft, 9 in.; 1.448 m.

Built by A. Robertson, Sandbank, Argyll in 1908.

*Galma* represents the changeover from steam yachts to motor cruisers. Designers faced many of the same problems at the changeover as they had with the coming of steam yachts. These difficulties included the lack of good horse-power from the size and weight of the machinery available, and the worry of head winds and rough seas, when only a limited power was available from the engines. When conditions were severe, it was sometimes impossible to keep making forward progress. If there was no handy harbour, ships would have to anchor, sometimes on a lee shore. This explains why yachts of this type carried anchors which are so large by current standards. They also had long heavy anchor chains, duplicated port and starboard.

However, by 1908, engines were reliable enough for designers to dispense with auxiliary sails, especially when there were two engines, as in this yacht. Each of the three-cylinder Gardner petrol/paraffin engines

only put out 50 hp, running at the subdued speed of just 500 revs per minute. This had one special advantage, these engines were relatively quiet, especially as they were in their own spacious engine room, separated from the saloon by two bulkheads, the forward one of which had no door through. Noise travels easily through quite small holes, so a solid bulkhead without even a tiny aperture through it is a good noise blocker.

The engine room looks vast, because it is, with walking space all around the machinery and full headroom. Six big skylight panels supply lots of daylight and, all in all, the engineer aboard this vessel has a much better life than his equivalent in many modern yachts, where there is scarcely room for tame mice to carry out any work. Gardner engines have always had a tremendous reputation for reliability because they were designed to keep running in adverse conditions far offshore. However, engines in the pre-1914 age did need plenty of attention. They typically had grease nipples and oil reservoirs that needed regular replenishing. Gaskets were not always reliable, so oil seeped out here and there, and any yacht engineer worthy of the name would regularly wipe over the gently pulsating machinery, ensuring no grime got into the bilge. Some owners insisted that their engines were enamelled white or cream coloured so that the tiniest drip of oil was easily seen.

When there is a shortage of power the only thing a designer can do is go for lots of length and the minimum beam. This explains the almost vertical bow to get the fore-end of the waterline well forward, the vertical transom stern and the relatively narrow hull width. The bottom of the transom is above the load waterline because, with these puny engines, there is not going to be any squatting of the hull when the throttles are right open. In later life, when more powerful engines were fitted, it is inevitable that the stern would sink somewhat under full power.

In the era when this yacht was built, owners and their guests wore smart formal clothes afloat. Men sometimes wore white trousers, and white shirts were very common. The detachable collars and sometimes detachable doubled cuffs could be changed during the day if they became soiled or tinged with sweat. The cuffs were often held together by cufflinks decorated with the owner's yacht club burgee in glossy enamel. Women wore long dresses, large hats and overcoats to suit the weather, all complex and costly. No-one wanted horrible engine exhaust smoke to sully such clothes, so there is a high funnel to dissipate the noxious smoke well above head height. This length of funnel needs four steel wire shrouds to hold it firmly in position – these obstruct the deck area, and also need regular maintenance.

The helmsman was out in the weather without protection, so when it was raining or there was a lot of spray flying about, he got wet, sometimes very wet. Some earlier yachts similar to this had the steering wheel aft of the funnel, so the helmsman could get a little protection from the spray by keeping in the lee of the funnel. However, it was necessary to take a look forward every so often to reduce the chances of hitting something solid, or being hit, so the chances of getting well soaked were high.

On the starboard side, this yacht carried a 12-foot gig for use by the owner and friends. On the port side there was a 10-foot dinghy for the paid hands. The side companionway, nearly always made of teak with gratings at the top and bottom, is naturally on to starboard because that is the side the owner always came on board. When not in use this elegant marine stairway was hoisted inboard using its own dedicated davit. The deck-plan view shows a ladder over the side, aft of the dinghy davits, for use by the paid crew.

At sea the yacht's boats had to be swung inboard for safety, and this made getting aft awkward, so when doing short fine weather trips the boats were left swung outboard hanging from the davits. They were tightly lashed to prevent them swinging about and efficient paid hands remembered to take out the bung in the bottom of the boat to let rain and spray drain away. Woe betide any hand who forgot to put the bung back before lowering a boat into the water.

A 'cat' davit was fitted near the stemhead to hoist the anchors up on deck. Before the coming of so-called patent anchors like the CQR and Danforth, the ground tackle was heavy. For a start, yachts built to Lloyds Rules had to have anchors which by today's standards are seriously overweight. It needed two tough professionals to recover an anchor when getting underway, even when using a davit.

Cooking was done in the foc's'le, so hot food had to be carried up the vertical fore hatch ladder, along the lengthy side deck and down the steep steps into the saloon. An experienced paid hand would know how to keep the food hot, by wrapping a thick towel round the bain-marie that held the food, with extremely hot water in the lower compartment of the food heater. The stove in the saloon would sometimes have a kettle on top, handy for making hot grog on cold Scottish summer evenings.

Aft there is a store as long as the saloon, but with no standing headroom. This sort of yacht needed lots of space for the deck gear like fenders and warps, buckets, boathooks and mops. Also, there is not much space in the foc's'le for stowing cooking utensils or food. Sides of bacon and nets of vegetables might be hung in this aft store, as well as spares, bosun's gear, tools and often lengths of timber and metal for mending everything on board. In well-organised craft, the paid crew would have a work-bench with a vice bolted to it for repairs and improvements.

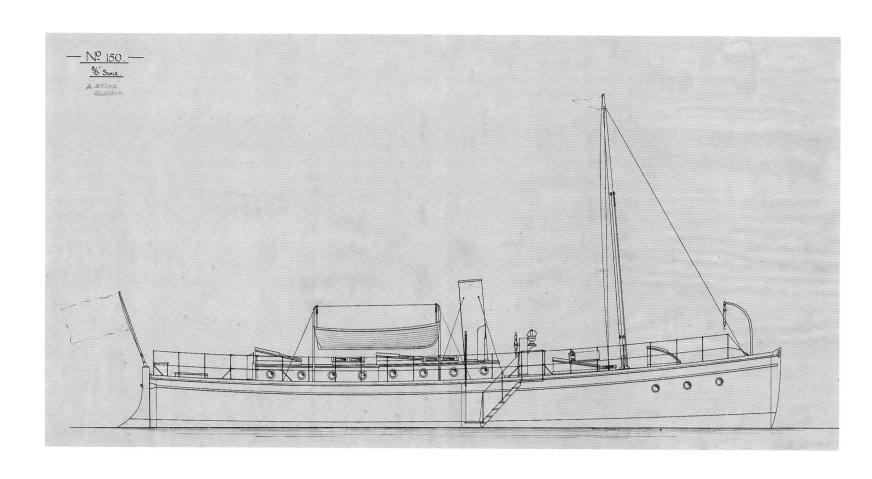

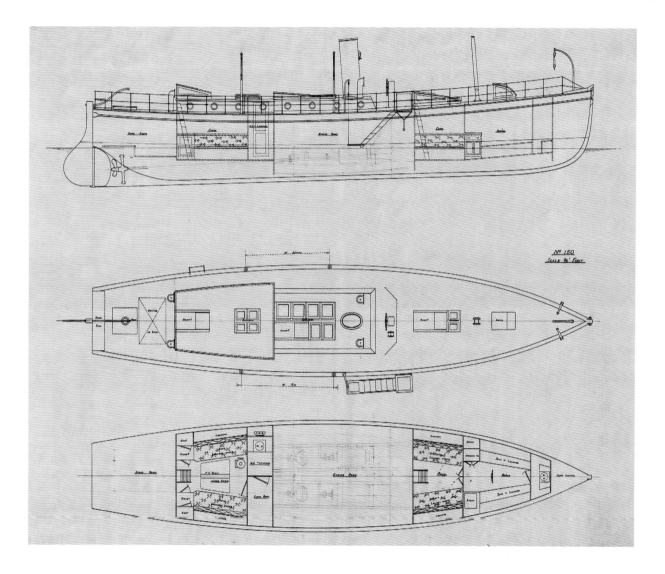

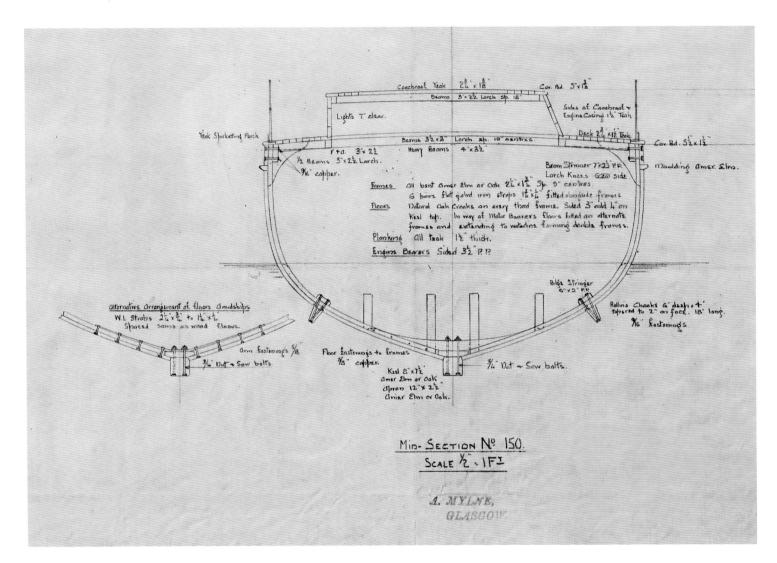

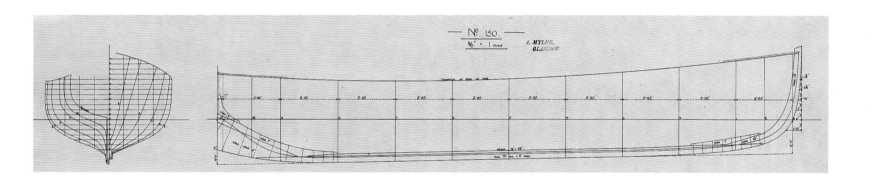

# CHAPTER 26

*Spanker* (later called *Lotos*)
Design No. 131
Length overall: 82 ft; 24.994 m.
Length waterline: 81 ft; 24.689 m.
Beam: 14 ft; 4.267m.
Draft: 5 ft; 1.524 m.
Built in 1909 by J. Reid & Co.
Engines: Originally twin six-cylinder Gardner paraffin units and later twin four-cylinder Daimler petrol engines.

It seems likely that the first owner of this yacht was an engineer, because about a fifth of the overall length is given to the engines. Access all-round the machinery is far better than in the majority of yachts, old or modern, and the furniture in the engine room might be called luxurious, what with the big work bench, long tool locker, twin lubricating oil tanks and two extensive shelves for the oil cisterns.

It seems likely that the engines were changed after very few years because paraffin may have been hard to get in German ports, but petrol was much more accessible. Changing engines would be fairly simple as there is a large skylight on the deck to lift them through. According to notes on the tank plan, the first set of engines used 4.5 gallons of paraffin per hour at 10 knots, giving a range of 660 sea miles.

The engines are 'toed in' at the aft end, so that the propeller shafts taper in towards each other as they extend aft. This has the effect of keeping the propellers well under the hull, where they are protected in harbours which have quays on sloping mud banks. Keeping the propellers well inboard also reduced the chances of them sucking foam or even air and hence loosing efficiency. By having the engines well apart there is room between them for maintenance work. A minor asset is that the further apart these heavy machines are, the less inclined the boat will be to roll, though this effect will be minimal.

Steel was used to build this yacht with a traditional planked deck. There were watertight bulkheads at each end of the engine room and aft of the chain locker. This type of bulkhead helps to contain the noise and reduce insurance premiums because it makes the vessel safer. A fire in the engine room will seldom spread beyond steel bulkheads. If the deck-head is steel lined and the fire is not too large, fierce or prolonged, there is a good chance it can be extinguished before destroying the vessel.

As there are two bulkheads between the saloon and the engine room (though only one is watertight), the owner and his family would hardly hear the chugging of the engines when under way, or the little generator when on moorings.

This hull was designed to be easily driven with little horse-power. There is no 'parallel middle body', that is, flat straight areas of topsides and bottom for much of the overall length, parallel with the centre line, as seen in most merchant ships and cheaply built craft. Instead, the hull is fine forward and the width grows gently outwards with the maximum beam considerably aft of amidships. The result is that the maximum beam is in the middle of the engine room where the main weights, the engines, gearboxes and big tanks, are located. When punching into waves, this yacht will rise and fall gently thanks to the fine forward sections and the way the principal weights are located well back.

It is unusual to have the crew accommodation right aft. Here, the skipper, engineer, deck-hand and cook would live through the summer. Fridays would be busy, getting everything clean and smart for the owner and his party arriving in the evening. The saloon stove would be fired up to ensure the forward part of the yacht was dry and comfortable. Smoke from this stove is carried up the mast and hopefully well away from the owner's party when they are enjoying good weather under the awning over the aft deck.

With so little storage space for food, a call on Fridays to the local butcher, grocer and greengrocer would be essential to get enough fresh food on board for the whole weekend. The owner's party could be up to seven people, but probably less, as the tables in the saloon and deck saloon were small for that number. Also, using the settees in the saloon for sleeping would be inconvenient except for short periods.

Typical of the time when this yacht was built, the helmsman has little protection from the weather, though he should often be safe from spray due to his height above the waterline. When manoeuvring, he would ring down to the engine room where the engineer would operate the throttles and gears.

The ship's boats were a 16-foot, or 4.88 metres, motor launch and a 15-foot, or 4.57 metres, gig. The latter is a light, narrow, easily rowed boat, often clincher planked. Before 1939 it was usual for most yacht's boats to be varnished all over, inside and outside, apart from below the waterline. This had lots of advantages over paint. Defects such as splits or rot can be seen as soon as they occur. Recoating is quicker as there are no paint edge lines to 'cut in', and quick-drying varnish is easy to obtain.

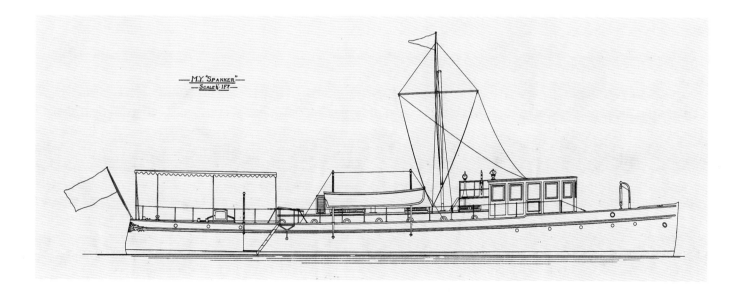

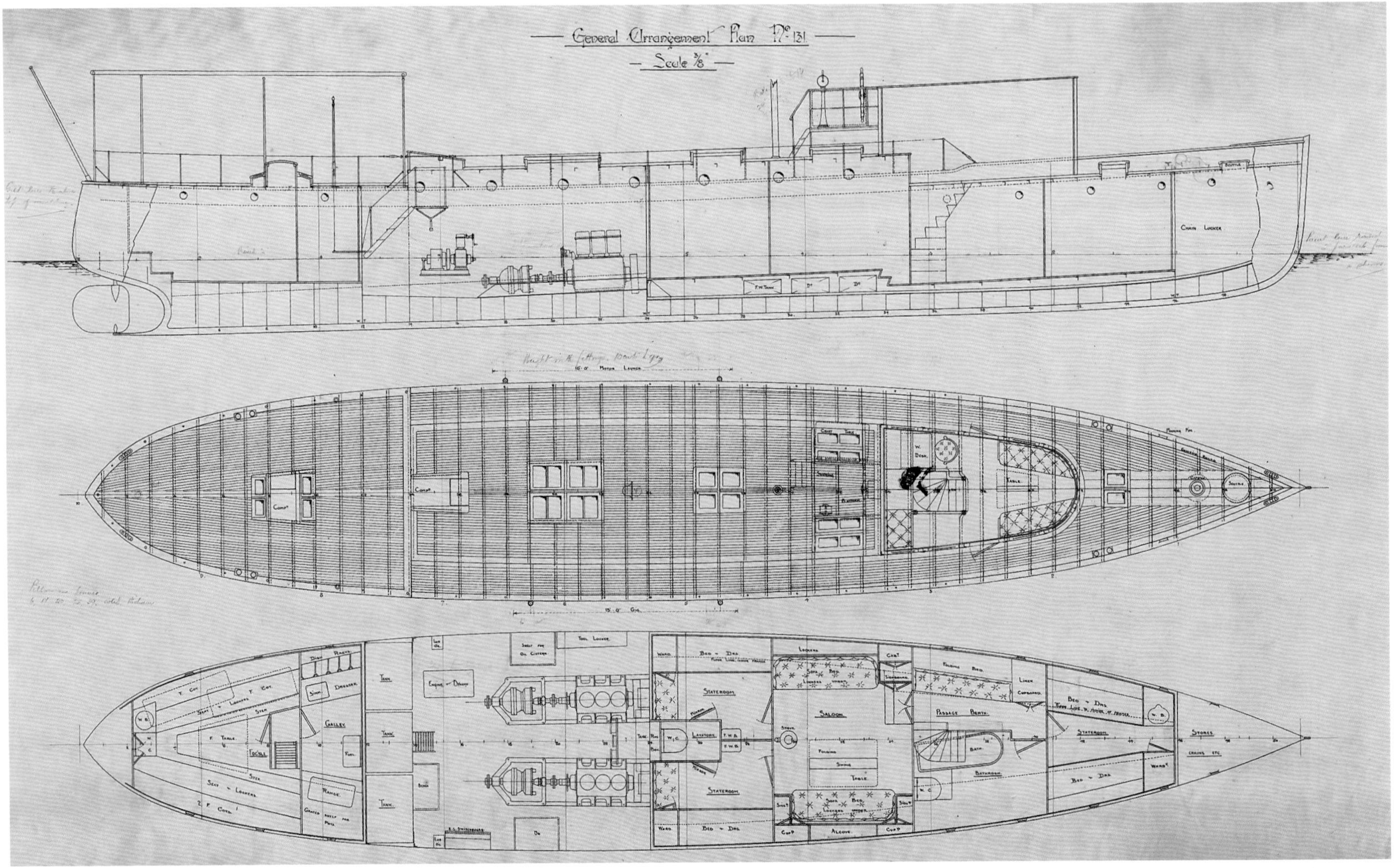
General Arrangement Plan No. 131
Scale 3/8"
Chain Locker
16'-0" Motor Launch
15'-0" Gig
Galley
Dresser
Range
Tank
Engine - Dinghy
Tool Locker
Stateroom
Saloon
Lavatory
Passage Berth
Linen Cupboard
Bathroom
Bath
Stores
Chains etc
Alcove
Bed - Drs

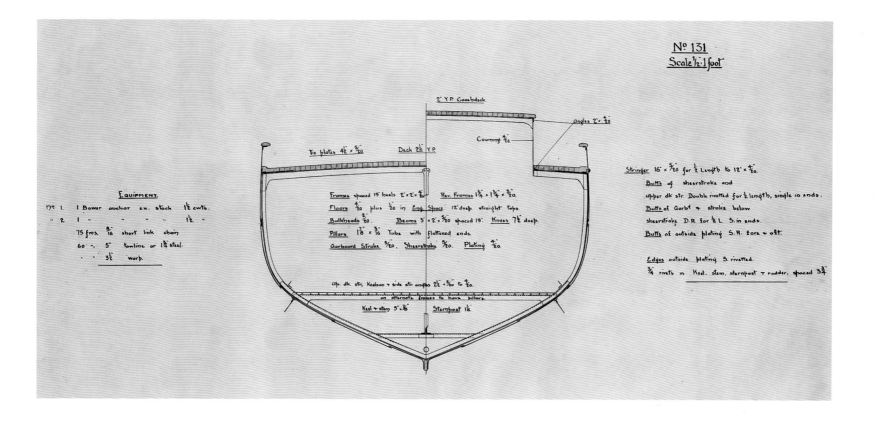

No 131
Scale ½: 1 foot

2" Y.P. Coachdeck.

angles 2" × 4/20

Coaming 4/20

Tie plates 4½" × 5/20      Deck 2½" Y.P.

Stringer 16" × 5/20 for ½ Length to 12" × 4/20.

Butts of sheerstroke and

upper dk str. Double rivetted for ½ length, single in ends.

Butts of Garb.d + stroke below

sheerstroke D.R. for ½ L. S. in ends.

Butts of outside plating S.R. fore + aft.

Edges outside plating S. rivetted.

¾ rivets in Keel. stem. sternpost + rudder. spaced 3¾

**EQUIPMENT.**

No 1.   1 Bower anchor ex. stock 1½ cwts.
"   2    1      "      "      "      "    1½ "
75 fms. 3/16 short link chain
60 ", 5" towline or 1¾ steel.
" " 3½" warp.

Frames spaced 19" heels 2" × 2" × 4/20.   Rev. Frames 1¾ × 1¾ × 3/20.
Floors 4/20 plus 1/20 in Eng. Space. 12" deep. straight tops.
Bulkheads 2/20.   Beams 3" × 2" × 5/20 spaced 19".   Knees 7½" deep.
Pillars 1⅞" × 3/16 Tube with flattened ends.
Garboard Stroke 5/20.   Sheerstroke 5/20.   Plating 4/20.

Up. dk. str. Keelson + side str. angles 2½" × 5/20 to 4/20.
on alternate frames to have pillars.

Keel + stem 5" × ⅞"      Sternpost 1⅞"

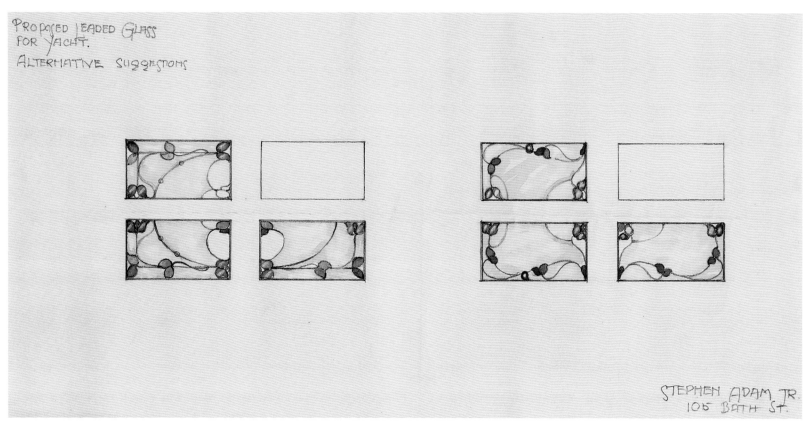

Proposed leaded glass windows for *Galma*.

# CHAPTER 27

*Sea King II*
Design No. 248
L.O.A.: 127 ft, 7 in.; 38.89 m.
L.W.L.: 123 ft, 6 in.; 37.64 m.
Beam: 25 ft, 6 in.; 7.77 m.
Draft: 5 ft, 6 in.; 1.68 m.
Speed 10 knots with two 220 hp engines.

This vessel might be called an expedition ship rather than a yacht. The owner, Henry Edward Ernest Victor, Baron Bliss, had her specially designed for his unusual needs. He wanted to live and work on board while exploring and fishing for sport in the Caribbean. This explains why there is a study and a business room on board. He wanted a yacht large enough to live aboard permanently in great comfort while making major cruises, and, as he was confined to a wheelchair, there was a lift between the decks. He insisted on being properly looked after, which explains why there was a paid crew more than double the number of the owner's party.

This yacht's lines are unusual, as there is an almost flat bottom and tight turn of the bilge, while the middle of the hull is almost parallel-sided, like a merchant ship. The shallow draft is a main reason for this shape. The long water line length and canoe stern suit the low power and modest top speed of 10 knots, but this gives a long range of 1,500 miles.

The engines were Petter VJ4 M diesels, each with an output of 220 hp. Though there are twin engines, there is a single rudder, probably to minimise complications and also reduce the building and maintenance costs. This vessel was not designed to turn tightly in cramped marinas, she was built fifty years before the first marina appeared. However, with her big outward turning propellers, one going ahead and one astern, she would turn quickly enough to get out of a tight harbour.

The layout is unusual in that the engine room is forward of amidships, but this is a feature found in several Mylne designs. The advantages include:

- Engine noise is well away from the owner's quarters.
- The heavy fuel tanks are amidships so the yacht's trim fore and aft does not vary regardless of whether the tanks are full or empty.
- The watertight bulkheads at each end of the engine room give a lot of athwartships strength and contain the machinery sounds.
- The shaft angle is more or less horizontal, which makes for propulsive efficiency and to a small degree can simplify the construction.

Normally, having the engines so far forward makes it difficult to get the exhaust gasses away without having long water-filled pipes running through the accommodation. However, *Sea King II* has a hollow steel main mast, which is divided internally into four channels. Two are for the exhaust pipes for the main engines, one is for the exhaust from the auxiliary engine and one is the funnel for the boiler. Clear of this hot tubular steel mast is the wooden top-mast, and at the join there is a traditional crow's nest with a handrail round and a teak grating for the lookout to stand on. If there was a strong wind from aft, this perch would be smoky and at times untenable.

Electricity is supplied by the auxiliary engine, which also works an air compressor, some pumps and the fridge machinery. To be doubly safe there is a hand pump for recharging the air bottles which start the engines.

A simple ketch rig is fitted but it will hardly drive this vessel, except in strong winds, as the gaff mainsail, mizzen and jib are all small. However, these sails will reduce the tendency to roll, notably by cutting down the arc through which the boat moves. The way this works is that the up-wind amount of rolling is minimised, so that in ideal conditions the boat will hardly roll to windward at all, and the downwind component is likely to be smaller. The mainsail is set without a boom, but there is a strong gantry for lifting the 26-foot (8-metre) fishing launch over the side. Anyone stuck in a wheelchair does not want a tiny boat when away from the mother yacht on a day's angling. This sizeable launch, as big as many yachts, will be comfortable unless the weather is horrible. Backing it up, there is a 17-foot (5.2-metre) boat and a 14-foot (4.3-metre) dinghy.

Wheelchairs take up room and need space for turning, so the owner's sleeping cabin is large and it has a recess which is not bulk-headed off, where there is a roomy bath and toilet facilities. Adjacent, there is a study and the main saloon which has an expanding dining table, a writing table, a card table and a tea table beside an L-shaped settee on the port side. There is lots of space in this whole area because the cabin sides are flush with the ships sides. In a wildly dangerous sea this can give extra stability when the yacht is in danger of being capsized.

When this ship was built, teak was not so very expensive, as it now is, at three or four times the price of other good timbers. She has not just teak for the keel, stem, planking and decking, but also teak beams, beam shelves and frames, which is unusual. The beam shelves are wedge-shaped, which gives good strength for the weight and makes the fitting of the many wrought iron hanging knees simpler and stronger. The less excellent part of the specification is the requirement for galvanised fastenings. These work well and last as long as the zinc skin is intact. However, when driving in a galvanised bolt, screw or nail the protective coating sometimes gets chipped and then rust is likely to begin soon and spread.

The cabin sole is pitch pine, another wonderful wood favoured because it is strong and holds fastenings efficiently. A delightful detail seen on the plans are the door sills, which are tapered on both edges to make the passage of a wheelchair easy. Unlike many modern vessels, this one has four anchors, the biggest being 952 lbs, or 420 kg. The kedge anchor is just 140 lbs, or 63 kg, so it is light enough for a skilled seaman to take off in the smallest boat if the yacht runs aground and needs to use this anchor to winch herself into deep water.

The design of any ship is a compromise, and here we see that the galley is right forward, where the crew live, but a long way from the owner's saloon. However, this yacht was designed for the tropics, so with care and skill the food should not have got cold between its cooking and eating.

Baron Bliss left a substantial sum of money to benefit the Caribbean country of Belize. As a result, each year there are regattas in that country subsidised by the Baron Bliss Trust. In the same country there is also a Baron Bliss lighthouse, which commemorates an exceptional yachtsman who lived and died on this unusual craft.

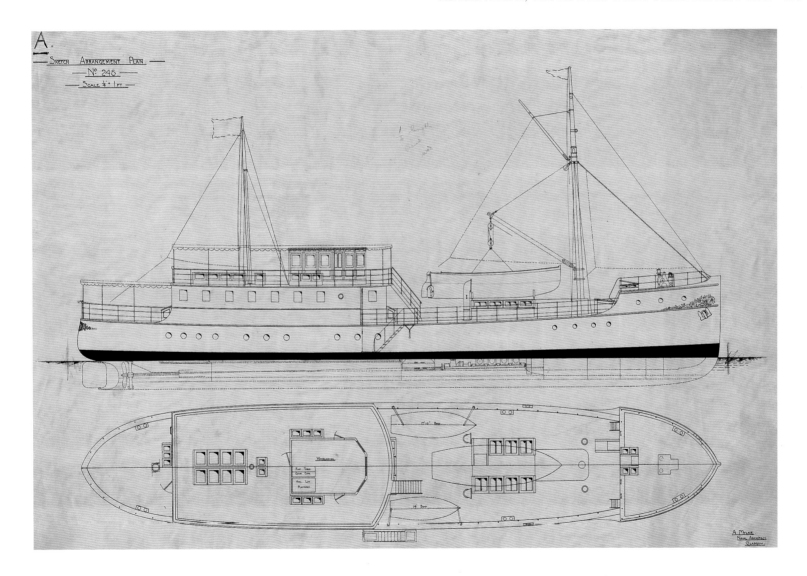

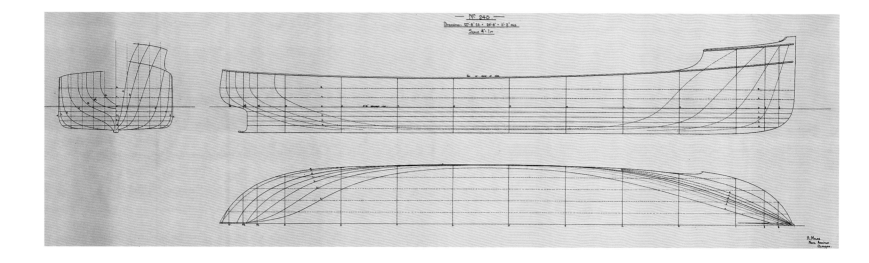

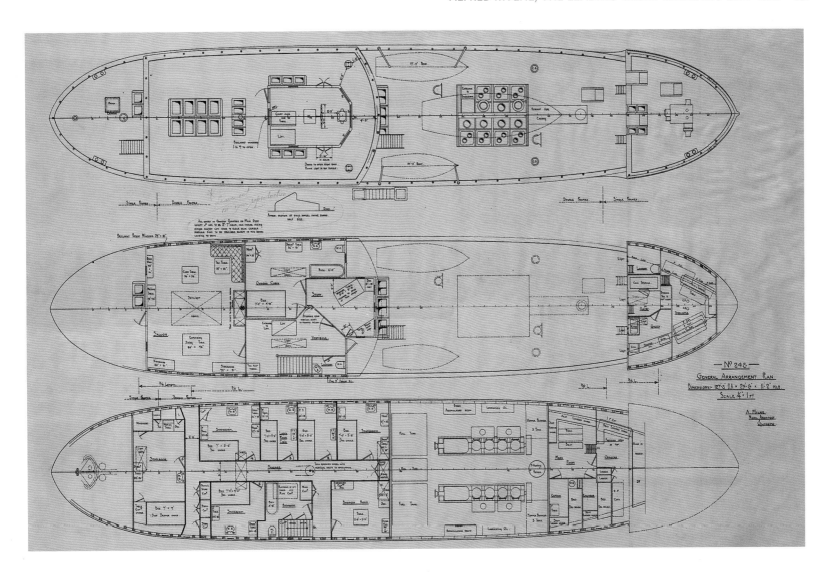

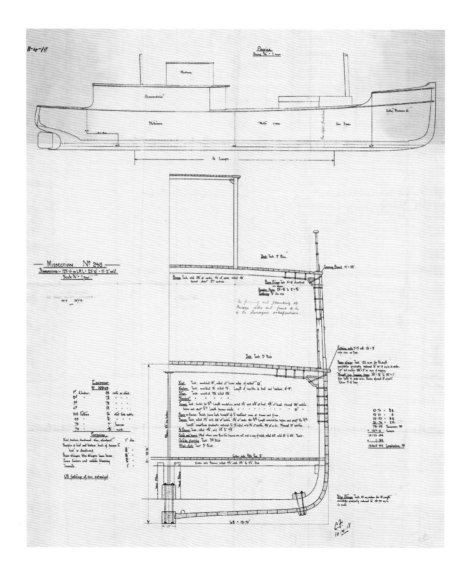

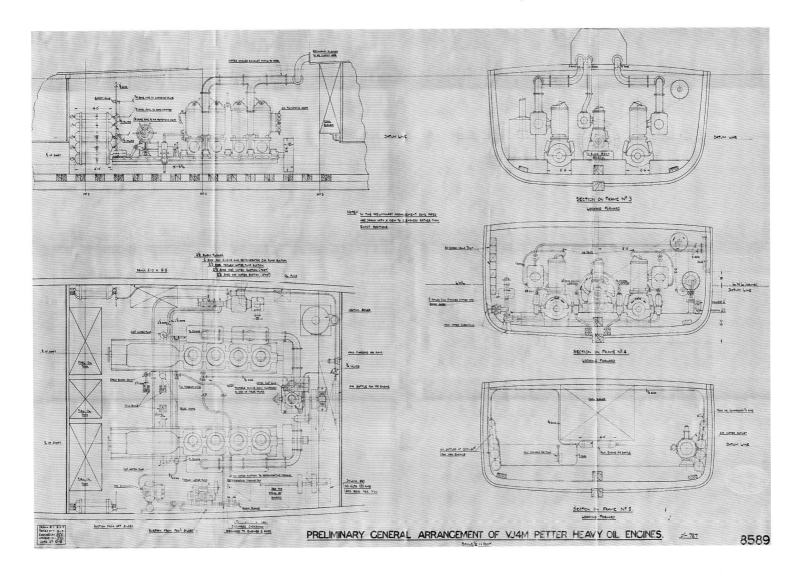

PRELIMINARY GENERAL ARRANGEMENT OF VJ4M PETTER HEAVY OIL ENGINES.

8589

Nº 248
Proposed combined steel mast and
Exhaust Funnel
Scale ·2· = 1 ft